JESUS OF THE BIBLE

DR. ED HINDSON

JESUS OF THE BIBLE

by Dr. Ed Hindson

ISBN: 978-0-692-38207-3 Paperback

Published by:
World Prophetic Ministry
P. O. Box 907
Colton, CA 92324

This book is based on the *Jesus of the Bible TV series* that was produced and directed by Mark Jenkins and edited by Larry Wheeler of Words of Victory Ministries in Richmond, Virginia for World Prophetic Ministry Inc.

This *Jesus of the Bible* book features the photography of Ben Jenkins and Ricky Gibson, as well as some stock and public domain photography.

Special thanks to: Nazareth Village, the City of David, and Sar El Tours.

TABLE OF CONTENTS

Introduction 5

About Your Teacher—*Dr. Ed Hindson* 7

Chapter 1   *His Miraculous Birth* 8

Chapter 2   *His Baptism & Temptation* 18

Chapter 3   *His Galilean Ministry* 30

Chapter 4   *Calling His Disciples* 42

Chapter 5   *Sermon on the Mount* 52

Chapter 6   *His Parables* 64

Chapter 7   *His Miracles* 74

Chapter 8   *His Kingdom & Church* 86

Chapter 9   *Answering His Critics* 96

Chapter 10   *Jesus Predicts the Future* .106

Chapter 11   *His Arrest & Trial* 116

Chapter 12   *His Crucifixion & Resurrection* 128

"...his disciples were with him: and he asked them, saying, Whom say the people that I am? They answering said, John the Baptist; but some say, Elias; and others say, that one of the old prophets is risen again. He said unto them,

But whom say ye that I am?"

LUKE 9:18B-20A

INTRODUCTION

H e is without a doubt the most influential person in human history. His radical teaching would shock and transform the ancient world. He has been called the Cornerstone of all of western civilization. The world's history is divided into ages before and after His birth. Nearly one-third of the world population—over two billion people—believe Him to be the chosen One, the Messiah from God. He claimed to be divine. He performed miracles. Witnesses said He was raised from the dead.

What do we know about this itinerant Preacher and Jewish Carpenter from a tiny mountain village in ancient Galilee?

Is He really who He claimed to be?

And what is His message for us today?

Follow Dr. Ed Hindson, noted Bible scholar, author, and teacher of religion, as we walk in the footsteps of Jesus in the land of Israel. Learn about the life and ministry of Jesus from the writings of those who witnessed it. Discover the Teacher, the Healer, the Prophet, and Savior, who would be called the Light of the world.

Discover Jesus of the Bible...

"I am the Resurrection and the Life."

Come with me as we go around this region from Nazareth to Capernaum to Bethsaida to Chorazin to all of the places where Jesus came, preached, healed, touched the lives of people, and ultimately...

changed their lives forever!"

ED HINDSON

ABOUT YOUR TEACHER

Dr. Ed Hindson is the Bible Teacher on *The King Is Coming* telecast. He is also the Assistant Chancellor, Distinguished Professor, and Dean of the Institute of Biblical Studies and the School of Religion at Liberty University in Virginia.

Besides teaching thousands of students each week, he is an active conference speaker and a prolific writer. Ed has written over 40 books, including *Final Signs; Approaching Armageddon* and *The Illustrated Bible Survey (B&H)*. He has served as the editor of five major Study Bibles, including the Gold Medallion Award-winning *Knowing Jesus Study Bible* (Zondervan) and the best-selling *King James Study Bible* (Thomas Nelson). He is co-editor the new 16-volume *Twenty-First Century Biblical Commentary* series on the New Testament (AMG).

Dr. Hindson is probably one of the most well-educated Bible teachers on the air today. He is a graduate of William Tyndale College. He holds the Master of Arts (M.A.) from Trinity Evangelical Divinity School and the Master of Theology (Th.M.) from Grace Theological Seminary. He also holds the Doctor of Theology (Th.D.) from Trinity Graduate School, the Doctor of Ministry (D. Min.) from Westminster Theological Seminary, and the Doctor of Philosophy (Ph.D.) from the University of South Africa.

Dr. Hindson has a gift for making complicated Biblical passages easy to understand for the average Bible student. Thanks to his experience as a university professor, he has a unique ability to communicate Bible truths to today's generation.

Ed and his wife Donna are natives of Detroit, Michigan. They have three children and seven grandchildren. Ed says, "My greatest desire is to lift up Jesus Christ and proclaim His Gospel to the entire world."

CHAPTER 1
HIS MIRACULOUS BIRTH

Location: Bethlehem Judea, Circa 4 B.C.

"*In the beginning was the Word, and the Word was with God, and the Word was God. The same was in the beginning with God. All things were made by him; and without him was not any thing made that was made.*"

JOHN 1:1-3

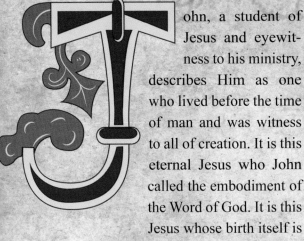

ohn, a student of Jesus and eyewitness to his ministry, describes Him as one who lived before the time of man and was witness to all of creation. It is this eternal Jesus who John called the embodiment of the Word of God. It is this Jesus whose birth itself is a miracle. He will enter this world with His birth to a young Jewish virgin in the province of Judea. Her name is Mary, and she has been called the most highly favored of women. She has been entrusted with the care of a Child that will be called the very Son of God.

The account of the birth of Jesus is recorded in only two of the gospels—Matthew and Luke. It is Luke who wrote this now familiar passage of Luke 2:11-14:

For unto you is born this day in the city of David a Saviour, which is Christ the Lord. And this shall be a sign unto you; Ye shall find the babe wrapped in swaddling clothes, lying in a manger. And suddenly there was with the angel a multitude of the heavenly host praising God,

Dr. Hindson overlooking the city of Bethlehem and the Shepherd's Fields

and saying, Glory to God in the highest, and on earth peace, good will toward men.

When the choir of angels assembled here at **Bethlehem** above the shepherds' fields, they announced, "Glory to God in the highest…for unto you is born this day in the city of David a Savior, who is Christ the Lord," and on that night, the glory of God returned to earth. He came in the person of a Baby, who was born in a box in a manger in a barn in a cave here in Bethlehem. In the photo above, I'm standing on the edge of the shepherds' fields

in Bethlehem. It is here in this little village five miles from Jerusalem that Jesus came to earth to be born as God incarnate in a human body. He is God who would walk among us.

The interesting thing about this place is that, when the wise men arrived in Jerusalem asking the question, "Where is the Baby who has been born King of the Jews? We've seen His star in the east," King Herod was thinking, "I'm the king of the Jews. That's my title given to me by Augustus Caesar." At this point, Herod was about six months from his own death. He was old and cynical. He was

Herod's Palace in Masada

paranoid and angry, and he was afraid that somebody—anybody—might take his throne away from him. In fact, he often had his own children eliminated and executed for fear that they might take the throne from him. He had some of his wives executed, as well.

Now, Herod heard these wise men say, "Where's the Baby born King of the Jews." Herod called in the Jewish scribes and asked them, "Where does the prophet predict that the Messiah will be born?" They then quoted Micah 5:2, *"But thou, Bethlehem Ephratah, though thou be little among the thousands of Judah, yet out of thee shall he come forth unto me that is to be ruler in Israel; whose goings forth*

have been from of old, from everlasting." The everlasting One or the *El Olam* was to be born here in this little town of Bethlehem.

There was only one other king who was ever born in Bethlehem, and that was King David. Every other king who descended from David was born in Jerusalem, and yet 700 years before the birth of Jesus, the prophet Micah predicted the Messiah would be born in Bethlehem.

> *The birth of Jesus is celebrated around the world by over two billion people each year*

The birth of Jesus is celebrated around the world by over two billion people each year. These celebrations take place on or about December 25th. The gospel accounts tell us much about the birth of Jesus—with one notable exception. We do not know the day or even the season that He was born.

This had led to speculation that Jesus may have actually been born in the springtime near

View of Historical Bethlehem

Entry of Pilgrims into Bethlehem at Christmas time, taken in 1890.

the time of the Jewish celebration of Passover, when the Jews remember their deliverance from Egypt. There is also speculation that Jesus may have been born in the fall of the year during another commemoration of the Jewish flight from Egypt. This is a celebration known as *Sukkot* or tabernacles. Like Passover, this is one of the pilgrim feasts that would have drawn Jews from across the provinces of Judea and Samaria to the Holy City of Jerusalem. With so many Jews already traveling, it may have made the census that Matthew and Luke speak about more feasible.

It may also explain why there was no room for Mary and Joseph in the inn, as Jerusalem and surrounding towns and villages would have been full of Israel's faithful pilgrims.

We may never know the reason that the actual birthday of Jesus has been omitted from history. We do know, however, that no other birth was as important or had more impact on history. As a young Jewish girl hushed the cries of her infant Son on that fateful night in the little village of Bethlehem, she held in her arms the most influential person who would ever be born. She named Him *Yeshua*, which in Hebrew means "the One who saves."

Luke's account of the birth of Jesus in the city of David, which is Bethlehem, fulfills many ancient prophecies regarding the *Mashiach* or the Messiah. Jews had long believed that a messiah would come to complete the law of Moses and lead their people to peace and prosperity. These prophecies are linked to both the place and the lineage of Jesus.

The gospel writer, Matthew, was sure to include a genealogy in his account to show that Mary and Joseph are indeed descendants of King David.

The Christmas story really began a thousand years before Joseph and Mary ever made their journey to Bethlehem. A thousand years earlier, in 1100 B.C., Naomi and Ruth made a journey from Moab on the other side of the Jordan River to Bethlehem, which was Naomi's hometown. It was here that Ruth went out to glean in a farmer's fields trying

> *The Christmas story really began a thousand years before Joseph and Mary ever made the journey to Bethlehem*

to pick up a few scraps in order to survive. There Ruth met her future husband, Boaz, the wealthy man from Bethlehem, who would fall in love with a Gentile woman and ultimately marry her. They are the great grandparents of King David. King David grew up right here

in Bethlehem, and he was ultimately destined to be the great king of Jerusalem, the great king of Israel, and the ancestor of Jesus.

That's why, when you open your Bible to Matthew 1, it begins by saying, *"The book of the generation,"* or genealogy, *"of Jesus Christ, the son of David, the son of Abraham."* It connects Jesus back to His Old Testament roots. He's the fulfillment of all those prophecies, pictures, and types of the Old Testament. The Old Testament is not divorced from the person of Jesus; it's integrated totally with the person of Jesus Christ. It's ultimately all about Him.

He would say to His own disciples that if you search the Scriptures, referring to the Old Testament Scriptures—the Law, the Prophets, the Psalms—you'll discover that it's all about Me. Think of it for a moment. God Himself stepped into the human race as a Baby born in a box in a barn here in Bethlehem.

Jesus was aware that King Herod, who was ruling in Jerusalem, was worried that somehow this Baby might take credit away from him. Herod sent the wise men to search

Herod's tomb in Herodium

for the Baby and told them, "If you find Him, send word to me so I can come and worship Him," but Herod really intended to kill Him. We know from history and from the Biblical account that King Herod died about six months later when he went down to Jericho by the Dead Sea to try to survive the winter months. Yet, he died anyway. An entourage brought his dead body back here to Bethlehem, and he's buried in the Herodium in that great mountain fortress.

For years, the Israeli archaeologist, Ehud Netzer, searched for the remains of the tomb of Herod, and after nearly 30 years of looking for it, he finally found the tomb. Today, the casket or sarcophagus of Herod is in the museum. It's proof that there really was a King Herod and really was an incident in which he ultimately tried to claim that he was the rightful king of the Jews.

Herod was ruling under Augustus Caesar and was really a puppet king, but he was a king who thought, "I am the king of the Jews, and I'm going to be the one buried in the mountain here." However, the real King of Israel was the Baby born in the box in the barn. There, the Child laid in the manger and was worshiped by shepherds.

Later, he was worshiped by the wise men, who arrived sometime after His birth and bowed before Him and acknowledged, "This is the real true King of the Jews."

Augustus decreed that all the world should be taxed, and everyone had to return to his hometown for the taxation. Joseph was the legal father of Jesus and husband of Mary, even though Mary was pregnant from a virginal conception as predicted by the prophet Isaiah in the Old Testament. Isaiah said that a virgin would conceive and used a unique Hebrew word *almah*. It's not the normal word used for virgin. It's a unique word that refers to a young woman of marriageable age who is indeed a virgin, a maiden. In other words, he picks exactly the right word to describe the virgin birth in advance.

Matthew, Jesus' disciple, while writing his gospel account, uses the Greek word *parthenos*

Shepherds' Fields over Bethlehem

in the Greek New Testament. This word always and only means virgin. In other words, Jesus' own disciple believed that the virgin birth actually took place and that it ultimately happened here in Bethlehem where the Baby was delivered. Now, Jesus was conceived by virginal conception back in Nazareth to the north. The family has to make their way from Nazareth to Bethlehem in order for Joseph to register for the taxation ordered by Augustus because Joseph's ancestors are from Bethlehem. It's here in this town that, when they arrive, she's ready to deliver the Baby.

You know the **Christmas story**. They go to the inn, and the inn is packed full because other visitors have come to do the same thing. I think it was out of kindness that the innkeeper said, "Well, at least there's the barn so that you're not out in the open somewhere," and she delivers the Baby in the barn.

There, the King of the universe was born in humble circumstances saying to each one of us, "I've come to be a Savior for all people." The Scripture tells us in Isaiah's prophecies that the Messiah would not come with elegance. He wouldn't look like a king. There would be nothing in the beauty of Him or elegance

of Him that would attract us to Him. No, He would come looking like a normal person.

He would be a simple, humble Rabbi, who would walk the hills of Galilee and dare to walk the streets of Jerusalem and even go to the temple itself declaring that He is *Mashiach*—the Messiah. *Yeshua*, His name in

Overlooking the city of Bethlehem (1898)

Hebrew, literally means Savior. It's like the English word *Joshua* in our translations.

Because He has come to be the Savior of all men, He came among men in this lowly, humble place in the little town of Bethlehem. Augustus' decree sends Joseph and Mary to the town just in time for the Baby to be born, and the angels' declaration is, "Glory to God in the highest for the Savior has been born here." The glory of God has returned to earth in the person of Jesus Christ.

The Church of the Nativity in Bethlehem

Think of it for a moment. God stepped into the human race as a Baby in a barn in a box because God loves us and God wants to become our Savior and Redeemer.

In the Book of Ruth, we read about the Redeemer, which is the *Goel* in Hebrew. This means to redeem or to act as kinsman. Ruth is redeemed by Boaz. He marries this Gentile bride who is a widow and brings her into the family of God. She's listed in Jesus' genealogy in Matthew chapter one.

Jesus is a descendant of Ruth and Boaz. You see, God was working His plan a thousand years before Jesus was ever born. In fact, God was working His plan, as we've seen, from eternity past that the eternal Word or the *Logos* would become a man and would take flesh upon Himself in blood and bones. He would live among men, but He would live above because, though He looks like a man, He's really God incarnate in human flesh. He is fully God, yet He is fully man at the same time.

He understands the pain, the difficulty, and the struggle of every human being. He was tempted in all points just as we are, but the Bible says, "Yet without sin." Only God can do that. Only a divine Person can do that.

If there was anybody who had the right to believe Jesus really wasn't God, it certainly had to be his disciples. They spent over three years with Him. They walked with Him. They lived with Him. They talked with Him everyday. Yet, every one of them ends up convinced that Jesus is God incarnate in human flesh. Only God can walk on water. Only God can raise the dead. Only God, who comes in the Person of the Messiah, gives sight to the blind.

> "God stepped into the human race as a Baby in a barn in a box because He loves us and wants to become our Redeemer"

Jesus fulfills all the Messianic prophecies. He can make the lame walk. He can give sight to the blind. He can heal the sick. He can cleanse the leper. He can raise the dead because He is God in human flesh.

For us, it all started right here in Bethlehem on earth. In reality, it started in eternity past. Jesus doesn't have his beginning here. He is God the Son, who has always existed from all eternity. He is the eternal One, whose goings forth are from everlasting from ancient times. Yet, He would be born here in Bethlehem in fulfillment of the prophets' indication or prophecy of what would come in the future.

It's interesting to me that Isaiah, who predicts the virgin birth in Isaiah 7, and Micah, who predicts the fact that the Messiah will be born in Bethlehem in Micah 5, were contemporaries. They lived at the same period of time around 700 B.C. They were prophets who were given by God a revelation of what would happen in the future. They looked down through the halls of history, down through the tunnel of time, into the distant future, and they see the Messiah is coming as a Baby born in Bethlehem.

Yet, Isaiah will go on to say that not only will He be a Baby born of a virgin, but He will also be a Baby who is going to be called the Wonderful Counselor, the mighty God, which is the *El Gibbor*, the everlasting Father or father of eternity, and the Prince of peace, which is the *Sar shalom*.

The divine Child spoken of in Isaiah 9 is the virgin-born Child in Isaiah 7. It's the Baby who's born in Bethlehem in Micah 5. All of those prophecies together give us a picture of God stepping into the human race because He loves us and because He cares.

The announcement of His birth is made to humble shepherds, and yet later, the magi or the wise men of the East come and bow down before the Child. They also recognize this is no ordinary Child. This is the One who is the fulfillment of the ancient prophecies.

Those wise men must have had access to the Hebrew Scriptures from the Jews of the diaspora after the Babylonian captivity because it's in the Book of Numbers (24:17) that we're told a star will rise out of Jacob and that star will ultimately receive the scepter of leadership as the King. In other words, the appearance of the star will have something to do with the birth of the King. The Bible tells us that all of those things came together on that night when Jesus was born in this town.

However, I want to take you to another passage that's less familiar to most people in the **Book of Hebrews**. In the tenth chapter, we read this amazing account of what was going on the night before Christmas.

In Hebrews 10:4, the Bible tells us that the blood of bulls and goats can never take away our sins. All of that was done in anticipation of a greater Sacrifice that would have to come in the future. Then, in verse five, the writer says, *"Wherefore when he cometh into the world, he saith, Sacrifice and offering thou wouldest not, but a body hast thou prepared me."* This

passage looks down through the corridor of time into the distant past. It reminds us of the reason why Jesus had to be born in a physical body in the first place. Why did *Yeshua*, the Son of God, have to become the Son of man? It was so He might offer that body as a sacrifice for our sins because the sacrificial system of the animals could never take away sins. It only covered your sin temporarily, but the blood of Jesus Christ washes us clean from sin forever.

Hebrews 10:5-6 says, *"Wherefore when he cometh into the world,"* which we celebrate at Christmas, *"He saith, Sacrifice and offering thou wouldest not"*—you don't want an

animal sacrifice or another offering—*"but a body hast thou prepared me."* Why? It's because, *"In burnt offerings and sacrifices for sin thou hast had no pleasure."* This is quoting an Old Testament Scripture.

Verse 7 says, *"Then said I, Lo, I come (in the volume of the book it is written of me,) to do thy will, O God."* Jesus understands from the very beginning of His birth as an Infant in the barn that He has come to fulfill the will of the father. He understands this as a Child. Later, at the age of 12 while in the temple, He says, "I'm here to do My Father's will. Therefore, should I not be at My Father's house?" He understands the significance of who God is, who He is, who we are, and why He has come in the first place.

In Hebrews 10:9, He repeats, *"Then said he, Lo, I come to do thy will, O God."* Then it tells us, "He taketh away the first," which is referring to the first order of the Old Testament dispensation of animal sacrifice, *"that he may establish the second."* He came to establish the second order for New Testament dispensation. In other words, all of those sacrifices and offerings in the Old Testament were merely temporary. They were preparatory for the coming of Jesus Christ, the Son of God who would die in our place and bear our sins on the cross.

is a real person who lived in real history. However, we also want to ask ourselves: Why did He come? What does this mean to you and me? What application is there for our lives today in regard to surrendering to the will of God? Can we find the purpose of God that we might know that we are not just a speck of human protoplasm on the scale of humanity that will soon be forgotten?

We are people who are created in the image and likeness of God in order to have a relationship with God and so that we might know the will of God and the purpose of God for our lives. Jesus came into this world with purpose. He was born in a box destined to go to the cross…

so He can change your life forever!

So, even from the manger, you look forward ultimately to the cross.

Jesus would eventually be raised in Nazareth in a carpenter's shop using hammers and nails as His tools, while knowing the entire time that the very tools of His trade would one day be used against Him on the cross when He would bear the nails in His hands and feet and hear the hammer wringing and clanging against the nails. Yet, Jesus said, "I've come to do Thy will, O God."

As He wrestled with all of that in the **Garden of Gethsemane**, He asked, "Is there any other way than for Me to bear the ugly sins of all mankind? Nevertheless, not My will, but Thy will be done."

Jesus reminds us of the importance of surrendering completely to the will of God, and as we begin our study of the life of Christ, we don't want to just look at the historical issues related to the life of Jesus, though we will look at many of the those because He

CHAPTER 2
HIS BAPTISM & TEMPTATION

Location: The River Jordan, Circa A.D. 30

"*Then cometh Jesus from Galilee to Jordan unto John, to be baptized of him. But John forbad him, saying, I have need to be baptized of thee, and comest thou to me? And Jesus answering said unto him, Suffer it to be so now: for thus it becometh us to fulfil all righteousness. Then he suffered him. And Jesus, when he was baptized, went up straightway out of the water: and, lo, the heavens were opened unto him, and he saw the Spirit of God descending like a dove, and lighting upon him: And lo a voice from heaven, saying, This is my beloved Son, in whom I am well pleased.*"

MATTHEW 3:13-17

Bathabara baptismal site near where John baptized Jesus

oday, happy pilgrims who travel to the Holy Land are being baptized in the river Jordan. It is a practice that dates back over 2,000 years to the earliest followers of Jesus.

Baptism by immersion has its origins in the *Mikva* or the ritual bathing that was the practice among the Jews. Baptism would become an expression of one's faith and devotion to Jesus and His teaching.

To first-century believers, just as with those who follow Jesus today, baptism is a symbol of rebirth fulfilling Christ's admonition that one must be born again to the life that God wants for them.

The importance of baptism may have been further underscored by the fact that Jesus Himself was baptized. He would be immersed in the river Jordan by nonother that John the baptizer, a controversial preacher and teacher who railed against the political and religious authorities of the day.

New Testament writers describe John as, "The voice crying in the wilderness," associating him with the forerunner of the Messiah predicted by the prophet Isaiah.

Dr. Hindson in front of the Caves of Qumran aka the Dead Sea caves

There are **two major events** that take place during the life of Christ in the wilderness of Judah: Jesus' baptism and temptation. As you see in the photo, I was standing near the Dead Sea caves in the Judean wilderness. It's near here that Jesus was baptized by John the Baptist. Then, after His baptism in the Jordan River, Jesus then made His way into the wilderness for the 40 days of fasting.

You can see the stark contrasts in the landscape. There's nothing out there. The only place to get any break from the sun would be in one of the caves. Yet, Jesus spent 40 days there in preparation for the beginning of His earthly ministry.

As Matthew, the disciple of Jesus, began to tell the story, he drew an obvious parallel to the life of Moses—that Jesus, in essence, is the new Moses.

In the story of Moses, he flees from Egypt and ultimately leads the children of Israel out of Egypt through the water of the Red Sea into the wilderness and then up on the mountain to receive the Law from the Lord—the Ten Commandments. In a parallel sense, Jesus also comes out of Egypt as a young child. He eventually goes through the water of baptism in the Jordan River. Then, He goes into the wilderness and stays for 40 days. From there,

John proclaims the coming Messianic Kingdom, and John is perhaps the very first to recognize Jesus as that promised Messiah from God. John tells his followers that he baptizes with water, but the One who is coming after him, Jesus, will baptize with the Holy Spirit of God.

His Baptism

Matthew 3:13-17 shares the story of the baptism of Jesus, *"Then cometh Jesus from Galilee to Jordan unto John, to be baptized of him. But John forbad him, saying, I have need to be baptized of thee, and comest thou to me? And Jesus answering said unto him, Suffer it to be so now: for thus it becometh us to fulfil all righteousness. Then he suffered him. And Jesus, when he was baptized, went up straightway out of the water: and, lo, the heavens were opened unto him, and he saw the Spirit of God descending like a dove, and lighting upon him: And lo a voice from heaven, saying, This is my beloved Son, in whom I am well pleased."*

The baptism of Jesus marked the **beginning of His ministry**. The fact that He was baptized by John indeed linked Jesus to prophecy, but it also certainly linked Him to known radicals who would dare to speak against the political and religious authorities of the day. John would later be arrested and imprisoned as a political threat to the Roman Empire in Judea.

He goes up on the mountain to give the Beatitudes and the Sermon on the Mount. Each of the Gospel writers parallels the life of Christ to different events in relation to the story they were wanting to tell. Matthew, in particular, continually refers to the Old Testament because he was writing to Jewish readers. He wanted them to understand that Jesus is indeed the promised Messiah. He is the new Moses.

We pick up the story in the third chapter of Matthew's Gospel. Verses 1 and 2 say, *"In those days came John the Baptist, preaching in the wilderness of Judaea, And saying, Repent ye: for the kingdom of heaven is at hand."* This is a very Jewish message.

Remember John the Baptist lived and died before Jesus went to the cross, before the Day of Pentecost, and before the beginning of what we would call the church age or church era.

John the Baptist is in the line of the prophets of the Old Testament. In fact, Jesus said that John is the greatest of the prophets. John came in the line of Isaiah, Jeremiah, Ezekiel, and the great prophets of God. He came as the last prophetic voice to the nation of Israel. He was calling on them to repent.

Baptism for the Jewish people is usually done either in *Mikvah*, which is a stone tank, or in a river of rushing water as a sign of repentance, cleansing, and renewal. It's

Believers get baptized in the Jordan River

not usually a symbol of salvation like we emphasize in the Christian era. It's more of a symbol of a cleansing, repentant commitment to the Lord.

John was calling on the Jewish people to **repent** and prepare themselves for the coming of the Messiah. He was the voice crying in the wilderness, which was predicted in Isaiah 40:1. Matthew quotes that verse in Matthew 3:3 saying, *"For this is he that was spoken of by the prophet Esaias* (Isaiah), *saying, The voice of one crying in the wilderness, Prepare ye the way of the Lord, make his paths straight."*

It was here in this wilderness, in this desolate place, that John the Baptist carried out his ministry, very much like that of Elijah the prophet. That's why Jesus would later say in Matthew 11:7-15 that Elijah had already come in the spirit and type of John the Baptist. If you receive it, John is the one who was the voice of Elijah that comes to prepare the way for the coming of the Messiah (verse 14).

They were quoting from Chapters 3 and 4 of the Book of Malachi in the Old Testament. The very closing verses of the Old Testament (Malachi 4:5-6) say, *"Behold, I will send you Elijah the prophet before the coming of the great and dreadful day of the LORD: And he shall turn the heart of the fathers to the children,"* that's repentance, *"and the heart of the children to their fathers, lest I come and smite the earth with a curse."* With those verses, the Old Testament ends with a dull thud—the threat of the curse. The curse of what? It's the curse of the Law in the Book of Deuteronomy:

> If you keep the Mosaic covenant, these are the blessings that you'll have in the land, but if you disobey, these are the curses that will come upon you.

The ancestors of Israel said, "Yes, we will live by that covenant. We will live by that agreement." They placed themselves under that commitment, and the prophets came generation after generation warning them of the threat of the curse. The Old Testament ends with either the promise of blessing if you repent or the threat of the curse if you do not.

As the New Testament opens, John the Baptist came on the scene calling on the people of Israel to repent of their sins and to prepare for the coming of the Messiah. John had an incredible ministry with hundreds and hundreds of people responding to his message.

The people came down to the Jordan River for baptism. Then, Jesus Himself came. We see this in this unusual passage where the Bible says in Matthew 3:13-14, *"Then cometh Jesus from Galilee to Jordan unto John, to be baptized of him. But John forbad him, saying, I have need to be baptized of thee, and comest thou to me?"* John was saying, you don't need to be baptized. I'm not worthy to untie your sandals. I should be baptized by you. Yet, Jesus responded in verse 15, *"And Jesus answering said unto him, Suffer it to be so now: for thus it becometh us to fulfil all righteousness"*—I've come to fulfill all of the Law—*"Then he suffered him."*

The voice of God spoke as the Witness to testify to the fact that Jesus is no ordinary human being, but is the Son of God incarnate in human flesh

Jesus let John know that I haven't come to destroy the Law of Moses. I've come to fulfill the Law of Moses.

Then, John submitted and baptized Jesus, and the Bible says in Matthew 3:16-17, *"And Jesus, when he was baptized, went up straightway out of the water: and, lo, the heavens were opened unto him, and he saw the Spirit of God descending like a dove, and lighting upon him: And lo a voice from heaven, saying, This is my beloved Son, in whom I am well pleased."*

In the ancient world, to be the son of someone did not mean that you were less than your father; it meant you were of the same essence of your father. So, to be the Son of God meant that you were of the same essence as God Himself.

At that point, it was the **voice of God** that spoke as the Witness testifying to the fact that Jesus is no ordinary human being. Jesus is the Son of God incarnate in human flesh. He was walking among men, but He is going to live above men. He looks like a man, but He talks like God. He is fully human, yet fully divine. He was literally God on foot, God come down to this fallen planet in order to meet our needs.

His Temptation

Following the baptism, Jesus goes straight into this Judean wilderness. The Negev is the dessert of southern Israel, and you will not find a more inhospitable place on earth. It consists of rock, sparse vegetation, and heat. There is a large sea here, but the water is poison. It is a salt brine known as the Dead Sea.

In this Judean wilderness, Jesus prayed and fasted for 40 days after His baptism. He was tempted by hunger and by thirst, and according to Gospel writer, Matthew, Jesus was also tempted by the devil himself. During His self-imposed exile, Jesus was offered the world in exchange for His allegiance to Satan, the sworn the enemy of mankind.

After the baptism, the fourth Chapter of Matthew's Gospel says, *"Then was Jesus led up of the Spirit into the wilderness to be tempted of the devil."* Even though Jesus is fully God, you still see the ministry of the Father, who spoke from Heaven, and of the Holy Spirit, who directed Jesus into the wilderness. In addition, you see the obedience of the Son. All three Members of the **Triune** God are shown in action at one time. The Son was baptized in the Jordan River. The Father spoke His words of approval, and the Holy Spirit led Jesus into the wilderness.

Jesus was led of the Spirit into the wilderness to be tempted of the devil. Now, the Bible tells us that God does not tempt anyone to sin. However, God may

A view from Masada of the Dead Sea and the Judean wilderness

The Caves of Qumran where the Dead Sea Scrolls were discovered

sometimes allow circumstances to be set that will ultimately lead to Satan tempting us.

Jesus was brought into the wilderness for one key reason—to remind us that He's the sinless Son of God. Jesus is not just an ordinary human being who is able to resist the devil some of the time. He's the Son of God, who is able to resist the devil every single time. He alone can live a sinless life so that He could go to the cross and die a sinless death on our behalf.

Then, you have that **threefold temptation** that follows.

Matthew 4:2 says, *"And when he had fasted forty days and forty nights, he was afterward an hungred (hungry)."* I guess He was since He was out in this Judean wilderness in the middle of nowhere. There is virtually nothing to eat. There is very little water, except in a few springs here and there. Jesus was backtracking across this desolate desert area in order to prepare Himself for what lie ahead in His ministry.

We see several principles in this passage. First, we learn the importance of being in the right position in order to resist temptation. We learn the importance of fasting, self-discipline, and self-denial. This prepared Jesus to be able to deal with rejection and hostility, and ultimately, the self-denial enabled Him to go to the cross and say, *"Father... not my will, but thine, be done."*

The temptation is expressed in three areas. First of all, the tempter, Satan himself, came to Jesus in Matthew 4:3. Satan said to Him, *"If thou be the Son of God,"* so that's the issue. Is He really the Son of God? If so, then, *"Command that these stones be made bread."* Look at all the stones. You're hungry, even starving. If you're really the miracle-working Son of God, then turn them into bread.

I realize that, up til now, there have been no recorded miracles performed by Jesus in the Bible. So, whether He had done any prior to this or not, we don't know. There's no record of them.

Yet, this temptation was about **self-gratification**—do something to meet your need of hunger. Feed yourself.

Jesus won't do it. Instead, He quoted three times from the Book of Deuteronomy, which is the second giving of the Law by Moses. Jesus was connecting the Mosaic Law to His own experience when He said, *"It is written, Man shall not live by bread alone, but by every word that proceedeth out of the mouth of God"* (Deuteronomy 8:3).

> *The temptation of Jesus is expressed in three areas: self-gratification, self-glorification, and self-exaltation*

In other words, Jesus was saying, I'm being sustained by the Word of God, by the truth of God, and by the message of God, and I'm not being sustained at all by the food that I eat. Later, Jesus would sit down with the woman at the well in Samaria and say that He has water to drink that she didn't know about. His living water was to do the will of His Father.

He learned that lesson from a human perspective here in the wilderness.

Secondly, Matthew 4:5 says, *"Then the devil taketh him up into the holy city* (Jerusalem)*, and setteth him on a pinnacle of the temple."*

This was the highest point of the temple from where the trumpet would be sounded. From there, it is a sheer drop down into the valley below. There, at this pinnacle, the devil basically dared Jesus to jump off the pinnacle of the temple and prove that He is the Son of God. Then, Satan tried to quote the Bible to Jesus, *"And saith unto him, If thou be the Son of God, cast thyself down: for it is written, He shall give his angels charge concerning thee: and in their hands they shall bear thee up, lest at any time thou dash thy foot against a stone."* This is a quote from the Psalms, and Satan was tempting Him with **self-glorification**.

Then, Jesus looked at Satan and said, *"Thou shalt not tempt the Lord thy God."* Now, Jesus did not mean, "Satan, you shall not tempt Me." What Jesus meant was, "I cannot tempt the Father by doing something foolish in My human physical condition, like jumping off the pinnacle of the temple and expecting God to catch Me."

How many times do we put ourselves at risk in some foolish situation and then act like

God is supposed to bail us out? You might find yourself saying, "God, I've made all the wrong decisions. I'm in financial bankruptcy. Everything's going wrong in my life. So, God, bail me out." Maybe you've made all the wrong decisions in your marriage and in your family with your children, but then you say, "God, do a miracle and straighten it all out."

No, don't tempt God to go against His moral nature in order to help you or me get out of an immoral or improper decision that you or I have made. Jesus understood that. He basically told Satan, "I will not tempt the Father by doing foolish things that could cause a premature death." In the Bible, we call that the sin unto death. What is the sin unto death? It is anything improper that we do that can lead to an untimely death.

Ultimately, we're all gonna die. The Bible makes that very clear. However, when you do something foolish, such as drive your car too fast and cause the car to flip over, which ends up killing you in an accident, that can be a sin unto death. Had Jesus jumped off the pinnacle of the temple, it would've been the same kind of thing. Satan was trying to destroy Jesus. He knows he can't destroy God, but he might probably thought, "If I can destroy the incarnate One who is God in the flesh, I can

eliminate this whole challenge between me and God and all that is coming."

Satan knew that God had come to earth to meet the needs of people and to change their lives and their eternal destiny.

Finally, in desperation, Matthew 4:8-9 says, *"Again, the devil taketh him up into an exceeding high mountain, and sheweth him all the kingdoms of the world, and the glory of*

> "Satan knew that God had come to earth to meet the needs of the people and to change their lives and their eternal destiny"

them; And saith unto him, All these things will I give thee, if thou wilt fall down and worship me." In other words, I will surrender the kingdom of earth to You, if You will simply fall down and worship me.

That's what Satan has wanted all along. He wants to be God. He wants to rise above the divine One. He wants to be the one who

is the object of the worship of all creation. Now that he has the Son of God face-to-face here in this inhospitable wilderness, his cry to Jesus is, "Just worship me, and I will give you all the kingdoms."

In other words, Satan is telling Him that you can avoid all of the crises and all the conflict that are coming. You don't have to go to the cross. You don't have to die for their sins. I'll give this world to you. I will surrender it to you. This is the temptation of **self-exaltation**.

Yet, the Bible reminds us that this world doesn't belong to Satan. This world belongs to the Father. It was created by God the Father. It was given to the human race as a gift from God so that the sons of Adam and daughters of Eve might fulfill the mandate of God to literally lead this creation to be a blessing unto the Lord. All of the work that we do here on earth, all of the crops that we harvest, and all of the things that we produce in our culture ought to be a reflection of God's creative energy in our lives where it is an act of worship back to Him.

After this temptation, Jesus responded to Satan in verse 10, *"Get thee hence, Satan: for it is written, Thou shalt worship the Lord thy God, and him only shalt thou serve."* In other

Sunrise over the Dead Sea

you think you are? Only God can forgive sin." And, Jesus' attitude was, "Yes. Right. That's the whole point of all of this."

When Jesus stood trial before the high priest and was asked under oath, "Are you the Messiah? Are you the Son of God?" Jesus' answer was yes. Ultimately, we will see Him coming in the clouds in power and in great glory. Jesus knows exactly who He is. He understood why He had come to earth—to this fallen place—and that was to save souls, to transform lives, and to forgive sinners because He was heading to the cross to become sin for us.

One of the most amazing verses in the Bible tells us that He who knew no sin was made sin for us (2 Corinthians 5:21). Think about that for a moment. Here, in this Judean wilderness, Jesus ultimately resisted the temptation of Satan. The Bible says that Satan then left Him. The Scripture tells us elsewhere to resist the devil, and he will do what? He will flee from you (James 4:7).

We give into temptation so often because we do not resist in the power of the Spirit. We don't follow the example that Jesus set for us here in this wilderness.

Then, in Matthew 4:11, the Bible tells us that the angels came and ministered to Jesus.

words, I'm not about to worship you. I'm the One who receives the worship. I'm the One who comes as the Son of God. Ultimately, we know that Jesus is divine because He accepts and receives worship.

You'll occasionally hear people try to say, "Jesus never really claimed to be God. The church came along later and tried to deify Him and give Him a status He never claimed

for Himself. He was just a simple, humble Rabbi." Really? If that is true, then why did Jesus say, *"He that hath seen me hath seen the Father"* (John 14:9)? Why did He say, *"I and my Father are one"* (John 10:30)? Why did He claim the power to forgive sins (Matthew 9:6)?

His religious audience understood exactly what that meant. Those people said, "Who do

Now, if Jesus in his human incarnate form needed to receive the ministry of angels, how much more do you and I need to receive God's ministry in our lives? We even sometimes need the intervention of angels on our behalf and are unaware of this. You see, we are walking the journey—a path, if you will—through the wilderness of life itself. We face many obstacles, challenges, and temptations of self-gratification, self-glorification, and self-exaltation (or self-indulgence). In every one of those cases, the Lord wants to give you the power of His Holy Spirit residing in your heart, life, and soul so that you can resist temptation and live your life to the glory of God.

You say, "But, Ed, the Christian life is tough. It's hard to live." Well, ultimately, it's impossible to live unless the power of God Himself is alive in your life and in your heart. That's why, as believers, you have to first be **born again by the power of the Holy Spirit.**"

It's not self-effort that enables us to resist temptation. It's the power of the Spirit of God. Then, we have to be **filled with the Spirit as believers.** As the Spirit of God controls our heart, soul, and life from within, He manifests Himself without in how we live as believers in this wilderness life, if you will.

We too are on a journey or a pilgrimage. God has set us free from bondage, like He did with the children of Israel in Egypt. God brings us to the water of baptism at a time of confession of faith in Christ. Then, God ultimately takes us into the wilderness of resistance of sin. It is the journey of the believer, and this long sojourn path is what the Christian life is all about. It's not a hundred-yard dash. It's a pilgrimage. It is a lifetime marathon, if you will, of learning to live by the power of the Spirit of God, and eventually, we will reach the mountaintop of victory.

We're going to see this same pattern in the life of Jesus, as He goes from this place north into Galilee where He was from. We will see Him as He goes to the synagogue in Nazareth and dares to claim, "I'm the One who is anointed by the Spirit of God to preach the Gospel to the poor. I'm the One who is the fulfillment of the Old Testament prophecies."

As He goes into Galilee and calls His disciples and begins to prepare His ministry, He begins to train them to be ready to go and become fishers of men and share the Good News with the entire world. What Good News? It's the Good News that God loves you. Jesus died for your sins. He rose from the dead, and He's coming again.

That's the truth that will change your life forever!

Holy Land pilgrims circa 1920

CHAPTER 3
HIS GALILEAN MINISTRY

Location: Region of Galilee, Circa A.D. 30/33

> " *... by the way of the sea, beyond Jordan, in Galilee of the nations. The people that walked in darkness have seen a great light: they that dwell in the land of the shadow of death, upon them hath the light shined.* "

ISAIAH 9:1C-2

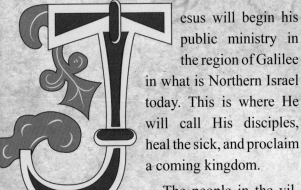

esus will begin his public ministry in the region of Galilee in what is Northern Israel today. This is where He will call His disciples, heal the sick, and proclaim a coming kingdom.

The people in the villages and towns of Galilee will be drawn by the thousands to hear what this Man has to say.

Was He the chosen One? Was Jesus the Messiah that the prophets of old spoke about?

Seven hundred years before Jesus was born, the prophet Isaiah proclaimed: *"...by the way of the sea, beyond Jordan, in Galilee of the nations. The people that walked in darkness have seen a great light: they that dwell in the land of the shadow of death, upon them hath the light shined"* (Isaiah 9:1c-2).

Many believe that the great light the prophet spoke about is the person of Jesus, and that His light would shine into the darkness of the hearts and souls of mankind.

Jesus began his public ministry in Galilee. After the time of the baptism and the temptation, we read in Luke 4:14, *"And Jesus returned in the power of the Spirit into Galilee:*

Recreation of a first-century synagogue located in Nazareth Village

and there went out a fame of him through all the region round about." The power of His preaching and teaching literally captivated people. They were astonished at His ideas and His doctrine because He taught with power and as One who had authority.

He has already been to Capernaum. Word has spread back to **Nazareth**, the town where He was raised in the carpenter's shop by Joseph. There, they want to know what the message is that has resonated so powerfully with people throughout the regions of Galilee.

When you study the life of Jesus, you realize that He was functioning totally within Orthodox Judaism of His day and time. He goes to the synagogues. He's not a revolutionary or a radical. He understands who He is, that He is the Son of God incarnate in human flesh who has come to fulfill the prophecies of the Old Testament. Luke 4:16 says, *"And he came to Nazareth, where he had been brought up: and, as his custom was"*—that means He went to the synagogue regularly—*"he went into the synagogue on the sabbath day, and stood up for to read."*

There is a recreation of a synagogue in Nazareth today at the Nazareth Village. It gives you an idea of what a basic synagogue

suffering servant who is crushed with the weight of our sin. Ultimately, in the Book of Isaiah from chapter 61 to the end of the book, He's the triumphant Warrior who is anointed of the Lord to proclaim the message of good news and to bring in the Kingdom of God on earth.

Jesus reads deliberately from the passage that we call Isaiah 61, and you can compare that in your Bible to the reading here in Luke 4:18-26. It begins, *"The Spirit of the Lord is upon me, because he hath anointed me...."* This is a Messianic passage. It's claiming the Messianic anointing on the person that Isaiah is talking about.

The Spirit has anointed Him to do what? *"...to preach the gospel to the poor; he hath sent me to heal the brokenhearted, to preach deliverance to the captives, and recovering of sight to the blind...."* Interestingly, there are no miracles of giving sight to the blind anywhere in the Old Testament. That is a unique sign of the Messiah Himself. When Jesus heals the blind, He is literally demonstrating the fact that He is indeed the promised Messiah.

prophet Esaias (Isaiah). *And when he had opened the book, he found the place where it was written."* In a moment, we'll read what He had to say.

This verse means that Jesus is literally and deliberately unrolling that specific scroll and going deliberately to this passage, which is toward the end of the Book of Isaiah. In our Bibles, it's Isaiah 61, which is five chapters from the end of the book.

In the **Book of Isaiah**, you're introduced to the virgin-born Child, who is the mighty God. This divine Child will come into the human race, but then He will become the

sides of the building itself. The men and women were separated from one another.

His Fulfillment of Scripture

It was here that a reader would go and pick up the Torah scroll or the scrolls of the prophets. In this case, Jesus' reading is from the prophet Isaiah. Luke 4:17 says, *"And there was delivered unto him the book of the*

The passage continues, *"...to set at liberty them that are bruised. To preach the acceptable year of the Lord."* In other words, He is speaking of the year of Jubilee when the debts are canceled and the captives are set free. Then, He stops right in the middle of the verse. If you look at this same passage in Isaiah's prophecy, Isaiah 61:2 goes on to say, *"To proclaim the acceptable year of the LORD, and the day of vengeance of our God; to comfort all that mourn,"* but in the **First Coming**, Jesus had not come to declare the day of vengeance. That's the **Second Coming**. That's the triumphant Warrior in the closing chapters of the Book of Isaiah, who will march across Edom in blood splattered robes as He splatters the blood of the enemies of God. He marches in triumph to

Armageddon to win the great victory of the end times. That comes in the Second Coming. That's not the First Coming.

Jesus understands that, so He stops deliberately in the middle of the verse because He's saying I have come to preach deliverance, to preach salvation, to preach the year of Jubilee, and to set the captives free.

Then, in Luke 4:20, we see that He rolled up the scroll, handed it back to the attendant, and sat down in typical first-century rabbinic teaching style. He sat down, and all the eyes of those in the synagogue were fixed on Him. There was something fascinating about Jesus and something irresistible about Him. When

Life as it was at the time of Jesus depicted in Nazareth Village

He began to speak, people would listen. They were captivated by His message, and they bore witness of His gracious words that proceeded out of His mouth.

The people wondered, "Isn't this Joseph's Son? Didn't He grow up here in Nazareth? This is amazing! Where did this come from?"

Then, in Luke 4:21, Jesus looked at them, *"And he began to say unto them, This day is this scripture* (Isaiah 61:1-2) *fulfilled in your ears."* Jesus is daring to claim, I am the fulfillment of the prophecy of Isaiah. I am the One who's been anointed with the Messianic anointing to proclaim the Gospel—the Good News. Not only does He go on to make that

announcement, but then, knowing what's in their hearts, He also says to them, *"Ye will surely say unto me this proverb, Physician, heal thyself: whatsoever we have heard done in Capernaum, do also here in thy country."* We've heard of the great works that you've done in Capernaum. What are you going to do here in Nazareth in your own town? In other words, do a miracle here, and then we will believe you really are who you claim to be.

However, He doesn't do it. Why not? It's because a miracle alone will not convert you. It may get your attention, and it may even draw your attention to the message that Jesus has. Yet, the miracle alone does not transform

a person's life. There were people who saw the miracles of Jesus and were genuinely saved, but there were many people who saw His miracles and still did not believe. Their lives were still not transformed. So, He doesn't do any miracles, but instead says to them, *"Verily I say unto you, No prophet is accepted in his own country."*

Then, He goes on in the sermon to make two points that they do not really want to hear. As He goes on in the application, in Luke 4:25-26, He says, *"But I tell you of a truth, many widows were in Israel in the days of Elias* (Elijah)*, when the heaven was shut up three years and six months*—in fulfillment of

Dr. Hindson at Capernaum in front of the Sea of Galilee

Elijah's prophecy—*when great famine was throughout all the land; But unto none of them was Elias sent, save unto Sarepta, a city of Sidon, unto a woman that was a widow."*

In spite of the many widows at that time, Elijah is not sent to any of those widows, except one widow in Sarepta, which is a city of Sidon up in Phoenecia in what today would be Lebanon. This woman is a widow who is a Gentile. In other words, Jesus was saying the only miracle that he did was on her behalf.

Then Luke 4:27 says, *"And many lepers were in Israel in the time of Eliseus* (Elisha) *the prophet; and none of them was cleansed, saving Naaman the Syrian."* Naaman also was a Gentile.

In other words, Jesus points to two miracles—one done by Elijah and the other by Elisha. Both of the people who benefited are **Gentiles**, *goyim*, or non-Jews. It's at that point that the people listening to Jesus got mad at Him. It really was not the fact that He was claiming to be anointed by the Spirit of God to preach the Good News. They're thinking that the Good News is to be proclaimed to us, certainly not to other people.

Luke 4:28-29 says, *"And all they in the synagogue, when they heard these things, were filled with wrath, And rose up, and thrust him out of the city, and led him unto the brow of the hill whereon their city was built, that they might cast him down headlong."* They would have thrown him down into the valley. The valley that surrounds the city of Nazareth is the valley of **Armageddon**. Think of the irony of that. You are going to throw the Lord himself into the valley of Armageddon where ultimately He will win His greatest triumph.

> *Isaiah tells us that the Messiah will bring peace to the nations and the Good News will not only go to the Jewish people, but to all people*

Jesus understands all of that, and He slips away from them and miraculously escapes. One of the saddest stories in all the Gospels is this story of Jesus' revisiting His hometown of Nazareth, where he is literally thrown out of the synagogue, not because He's claiming to be the Son of God or, on this occasion, because He's claiming to be the promised Messiah. Instead, it is because He's claiming that the message of the Messiah must reach and change the hearts and lives of the Gentiles of the nations. Yet, that's exactly what Isaiah says in his prophecies.

Isaiah tells us that ultimately the Messiah will bring peace to the nations, that the Good News will not only go to the Jewish people, but also to all people everywhere.

This is a convicting reminder to us who want to believe that Jesus loves us and has a wonderful plan for our lives, but when we see the Gospel going to people outside our racial background or our cultural comfort zone, then we question, "Well, I wonder if they really believe and if they really understand." Yet, I believe the heart of Jesus would again say, I've come to be the Savior of all people everywhere—the Jew and Gentile. I've come to be the salvation for both the black and white, the Asian and the Western, the Northern and Southern, the European and the African, etc.

The message of the Gospel is the same everywhere. God loves you. Jesus went to the cross, bore your sins, died in your place, and rose from the dead. Jesus offers you a gift of not only forgiveness, but also of genuine salvation and spiritual transformation. Ultimately, He offers the gift of eternal life itself. It's a question of whether or not you'll say yes to the One who says, *"This day is this scripture fulfilled in your ears."*

A recreation of a first-century carpenter's shop in Nazareth Village

The story of Jesus' life transitions from His experience in the wilderness with the temptation and baptism to His return to Galilee. Galilee is where Jesus is raised in the town of Nazareth, an obscure village where God could leave the Son of God protected, safe, and secure from harm in His early years.

Jesus is raised in the **carpenter's shop** as the legal Son of Joseph. The Bible makes it very clear, though, that He's the physical Son of Mary in the virginal conception and birth, but because of the marriage of Joseph and Mary, Jesus' legal father is Joseph.

We don't know a lot about Joseph from the Biblical account, but we know that he was Jewish. We know that he was a hard-working man, and we know that he was a carpenter, and he either worked with tools of wood or stone or both. He was what we would call a blue-collar worker. Jesus is raised in that environment to love and appreciate family, hard work, personal discipline, and his Jewish heritage.

It's that heritage that God will use when the Spirit of God enters into Jesus' life, and the Spirit of God baptizes Him, if you will, into the ministry that God has for Him.

One of the challenges in understanding the triune nature of God is that the Father literally leads Jesus in His humanity. The Spirit of

His Early Years

First-century Nazareth is a good place to settle if you want to disappear. It's a remote mountaintop village that is far from the political and religious center of Jerusalem. This is where Joseph will bring his wife and his adopted son, Jesus.

Mary and Joseph will make a new life here as they raise this Child that they knew is born of God to save His people.

Almost nothing is known about the childhood of Jesus. For the most part, the Gospel writers reported on Jesus' life after He began His ministry. There are many legends and extra Biblical writings that attempt to fill in this period of Jesus' life, but we can only speculate. We do know that Jesus returns to His hometown after His baptism and His time of prayer and fasting in the wilderness only to be rejected by the people who knew Him as the carpenter's Son.

God empowers Jesus, and yet He is always the Son of God. Even though He looks like a man, works like a man, and walks like a man, He lives above men because He's really God incarnate in human flesh. We know that from His words, His wisdom, His miracles, and His incredible sinless life.

There's never been a person like Jesus. He's not just one of the great religious teachers of all time; He is the greatest of all time because He is uniquely God the Son. He declares that about Himself. He understands that He's the Messiah, anointed by the Spirit of God to declare the Word of God. He knows that He's the Son of God and that He must be about His Father's business. He knows that He's also the Son of man—fully human, yet fully divine in order to accomplish the purpose to which God called Him. His training began here in Nazareth in a carpenter's shop.

His Time in Capernaum

At the time of Jesus, Capernaum is a prosperous fishing village on the shore of the freshwater lake known as the Sea of Galilee. Capernaum is a well-developed village with many homes and public buildings, including a beautiful synagogue near the shoreline.

Capernaum has a population large enough to warrant a Roman presence. Gospel writers speak of a centurion stationed in this village as a representative of the Roman authority in Judea. Capernaum is also the home of Peter, and it's where Jesus will establish His headquarters as He conducts His ministry in Galilee. Capernaum will be witness to more miracles than any other place described in the Bible.

Luke 4:30 tells us that He left Nazareth. At that time, Jesus comes back to Capernaum, and Luke 4:31 says, *"And came down to Capernaum, a city of Galilee, and taught them on the sabbath days."* That means that Jesus

Sea of Galilee as seen from St. Peter's Primacy

> Jesus looks like a man, works like a man, and walks like a man, but He lives above men because He is really God incarnate in human flesh

JESUS OF THE BIBLE

White Synagogue exterior

was here in this synagogue in Capernaum. You can stand in the remains of the third-century synagogue that was built right on the foundation of the **first-century synagogue** of Jesus' time. In other words, this is one place in Israel where you can say, "I've walked today where Jesus walked in this city."

Then the Bible says in Luke 4:33-34, *"And in the synagogue there was a man, which had a spirit of an unclean devil* (demon possessed)*, and cried out with a loud voice,* *Saying, Let us alone; what have we to do with thee, thou Jesus of Nazareth?*—in other words, this man knows exactly who Jesus is—*art thou come to destroy us?*—by using the terms we and us, the implication is that the man is possessed of many demons—*I know thee who thou art; the Holy One of God."* The amazing thing in the Bible is that the demons know who Jesus is. The blind know who Jesus is when they cry out, "Son of David, have mercy upon us."

The challenge is, when will the leaders know? When will they finally understand that Jesus really is *HaMashiach*, the Messiah, that He's the promised One, that He's the Savior?

Luke 4:35-37 goes on to say, *"And Jesus rebuked him, saying, Hold thy peace, and come out of him. And when the devil had thrown him in the midst, he came out of him, and hurt him not*—when Jesus commanded the unclean spirits to come out, the demons immediately came out of the man without harming him—*And they were all amazed, and spake among themselves, saying, What a word is this! for with authority and power he commandeth the unclean spirits, and they come out. And the fame of him went out into every place of the country round about."*

Now, Jesus didn't come just to promote Himself by any means or to spread his fame. The people did that automatically. What I love about these stories is that we see Jesus as God in action here on earth. His heart goes out to people who are sick, people who are dying, people who are threatened by disease, people who are possessed of demons, and people who are mentally disturbed. Here is a Savior who loves you. He has concern and compassion for people and reaches out to meet us at the depth of our greatest needs.

White Synagogue interior

The house of Peter

What a wonderful privilege it is to be in Israel today and literally stand in some of the very places where Jesus Himself stood. It's overwhelming to imagine the power of His presence and the irresistible nature of the influence of His teaching, of His miraculous abilities, and of His incredible compassion.

A Savior with that kind of love and that kind of compassion deserves our love our compassion, as well as our devotion. The real question is, does He deserve our **worship**?

Jesus clearly accepts and receives worship in the New Testament. If He were not God incarnate in human flesh, that would be an act of blasphemy. When He says to people, "Your sins are forgiven," the religious leaders of that time said, "Who do you think you are? Only God can forgive sins." That's exactly the point that Jesus is making. He is literally claiming to be God. Later, He will say, "Is it easier for Me to just say the words that your sins are forgiven, or is it easier to say to a crippled person to rise up and walk? Just so you will know that the Son of man has power to forgive sins, I say to you, rise up and walk" (a paraphrase of Mark 2:1-12).

Jesus is going to heal people with withered hands. He's going to heal people who have been lifelong cripples. He's going to heal

The Bible says that, after the service, they left the synagogue and went to Peter's house, which was nearby. Today, there's a covering over that spot. There was a small Byzantine church there in the Roman Christian era marking the spot as a significant place because it was where Peter stayed.

Luke 4:38-39 says, *"And he arose out of the synagogue, and entered into Simon's* (Peter) *house. And Simon's wife's mother was taken with a great fever; and they besought him for her. And he stood over her, and rebuked the fever; and it left her: and immediately she arose and ministered unto them."* Another healing that is so dramatic, so total, and so complete that she's instantly cured. Here He reaches out to the mother-in-law of His disciple, just as He's reached out to strangers and to the Jewish people who lived here in Capernaum and who came to this synagogue to worship.

people who have been blind their entire lifetime. All of those miracles shout to you that He is fulfilling the signs of the Messiah.

That's why, when John the Baptist was arrested and was facing execution while being held in Herod's fortress at Machaerus, which is in Jordan today, John sends a message to Jesus by some of his disciples. John's message basically asks, "You are the promised One, right? I do have this correct, don't I?" Jesus told them to go back and tell John that the blind see; the lame walk; the deaf hear; and the poor have the Gospel preached unto them. Those are signs of the Messiah and signs of that passage in Luke 4 that quotes Isaiah 61.

In other words, Jesus is reminding John of the Book of Isaiah and reminding John, "These are the prophecies, and I am the fulfillment." That Savior, who had been prophesied about hundreds of years in advance, had come. The Bible says that He is made of a woman and made under the Law in the right time exactly to fulfill the purposes of God.

Jesus can come into your heart and life at *exactly* the right time in order to meet your needs and fulfill His purpose for you!

CHAPTER 4
CALLING HIS DISCIPLES

Location: Region of Galilee, Circa A.D. 30/33

> *Now when he had left speaking, he said unto Simon, Launch out into the deep, and let down your nets for a draught. And Simon answering said unto him, Master, we have toiled all the night, and have taken nothing: nevertheless at thy word I will let down the net.*

LUKE 5:4-5

'm sitting on the side of the street of ancient Bethsaida in the photo to the right. It took the archeologists years to find this exact location. This is the town where Peter and Andrew and Phillip were from. The story of the Bible is about real people in real place, and this is one of those places. You can walk today on this first-century street, and you can know that you are walking where Jesus walked and where the disciples walked. It was here in Bethsaida that Jesus would begin to declare that He is the Savior, the Messiah, and the Son of God.

Jesus will begin His years of ministry in Galilee. Here, as He moves from village to village teaching in the synagogues, He attracts many followers, and yet He will chose only 12 men to become His trusted inner circle. These men will become known as the **disciples**. They are essentially the students of Jesus. He will spend the majority of His time teaching them the true nature of the living God. Jesus will prepare them to carry a message of redemption to the world.

The calling of the disciples is recorded in all four of the Gospel narratives, and it is Luke 5:1-3 that is perhaps the most eloquent account. *"And it came to pass, that, as the people pressed upon him to hear the word of God, he stood by the lake of Gennesaret, And saw two ships standing by the lake: but the fishermen were gone out of them, and were washing their nets. And he entered into one of the ships, which was Simon's, and prayed him that he would thrust out a little from the land. And he sat down, and taught the people out of the ship."*

As the people gather around on the shore, Jesus is sitting in the boat. His voice is reverberating off the water. It's like a natural amphitheater to speak to the crowd, and He sits down in typical rabbinic teaching style and teaches the people.

When He finishes, He then turns to Peter and says, *"Launch out into the deep, and let down your nets for a draught* (catch).*"* Peter, who is a professional fisherman, reminds Him that they had fished all night and caught nothing. In other words, you're good at teaching Jesus, but I'm good at fishing—that's my business.

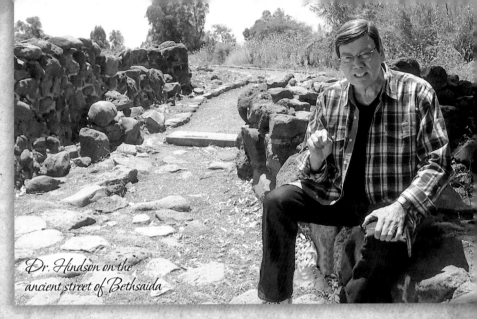

Dr. Hindson on the ancient street of Bethsaida

That's how I make my living. This isn't even the right time of day to catch fish.

Yet, Jesus has told him, "Peter, launch out into the deep." Again, there is something irresistible about the person of Jesus Christ, so Peter did what He said, *"Nevertheless at thy word I will let down the net."*

Jesus wants to take Peter deeper in his relationship with the Savior. He wants to help Peter understand that there's more to life than Jesus just simply blessing Peter's fishing business. He wants to teach Peter that He's going to make each of them a fisher of men.

The fishermen take the boat out deeper. They throw down the net, and immediately there is a huge catch of fish. The catch is so big that the nets are overwhelmed. Peter just

The Sea of Galilee near the location where the disciples were called

keeps pulling in load after load after load of fish. Luke 5:6-8 says, *"And when they had this done, they inclosed a great multitude of fishes: and their net brake. And they beckoned unto their partners, which were in the other ship, that they should come and help them. And they came, and filled both the ships, so that they began to sink. When Simon Peter saw it, he fell down at Jesus' knees, saying, Depart from me; for I am a sinful man, O Lord."*

The catch is so big that Peter realizes this does not normally happen. This is not a natural phenomenon. This is a miracle from God. As a result, Peter asks for his partners in the other boat to help him bring in the load of fish. When they finally get it all done, the boats are so overloaded that they virtually begin to sink. At that point, Peter falls on his knees and says to Jesus, *"Depart from me; for I am a sinful man, O Lord."*

Peter now recognizes the **supernatural** nature of Christ. He also recognizes the power of God that is on his heart, life, and soul. Peter realizes his own inadequacy like all of us do when we get closer to God. The closer we are to His holiness, the more we realize our unholiness and ungodliness.

Like every true believer, in that moment, Peter falls on his knees and says, "Lord, I cannot save myself." Peter is not saying get away from me. What he is saying is, "I don't deserve to be in your presence."

Then, the Bible says in Luke 5:9-10, *"For he was astonished, and all that were with him, at the draught of the fishes which they had taken: And so was also James, and John, the sons of Zebedee, which were partners with Simon. And Jesus said unto Simon, Fear not; from henceforth thou shalt catch men."* Jesus is saying, "I will make you fishers of men." That was a concept they understood. You have to properly cast the net; you have to be in the right place at the right time. You have to haul in the catch, etc. God is now going to use these men to haul in the catch of the other men who will come to faith in Jesus as Lord and Messiah.

Luke 5:11 goes on to say, *"And when they had brought their ships to land, they forsook all, and followed him."* That's the call of discipleship. Jesus calls all of us by saying, "Follow Me. Put aside every other commitment and every other convenience in life. It's all about Me and you. It's about your personal relationship to Me."

He didn't just say, "Follow My teachings." That's certainly part of it because His teachings were amazing. He didn't just say, "Be amazed at My miracles," because His miracles were incredible. What He's really saying is, "Follow Me." He will later say in John 14:6, *"I am the way, the truth, and the life: no man cometh unto the Father, but by me."* Now, if Jesus had simply said, "I am the Way; follow the way of life that I am modeling for you," then we would have to literally try to live like Him every single day of our lives.

Dr. Hindson on the shore of the Sea of Galilee

He could have just said, "I am the Truth, so believe this," but He goes beyond all of that to say, "I am not only the Way to follow; I am not only the Truth to believe; but I am also the Life that will change your life." This is because when the Spirit of God enters into the believer, then the Spirit of Christ comes into you, as well, and your heart is regenerated by the power of God. At that point, you have the ability to live like Jesus lived, to believe the truth, and to act out the truth.

You see, the message of the Gospel is a message of **head, heart, and hands**. God wants to inform the mind. As we look at the Parables of Jesus, they are all about understanding the truth so that you can believe the truth. The message of the Gospel is also about the heart so that you will love the Lord your God with all your heart, soul, and mind, as well as to love your neighbor as yourself. God wants to change your thinking so He can change your heart. Then, from the heart, we might serve Him with genuine love and commitment and compassion, like Jesus had.

Then finally, He wants to use our hands to serve Him. We, too, are to go forth and use our hands as an act of service unto the Lord. So, as God speaks to your mind and your heart, as He challenges your hands, what are you going to do for the cause of Christ to make it real in your life, to make it real in your generation, and to make a difference in the world in which you live?

Jesus will eventually call 12 disciples, and initially, He will send them on a mission that is only to what Jesus called "the lost sheep of the house of Israel."

Take your Bible, if you will, and turn to the Gospel of Matthew. There, in Matthew 10:1-4, we read the account that says, *"And when he had called unto him his twelve disciples, he gave them power against unclean spirits,*

Fisherman on the Sea of Galilee

Arbel overlook of the Sea of Galilee

to cast them out, and to heal all manner of sickness and all manner of disease. Now the names of the twelve apostles are these; The first, Simon, who is called Peter, and Andrew his brother; James the son of Zebedee, and John his brother; Philip, and Bartholomew; Thomas, and Matthew the publican* (or public servant; the tax collector who got saved at Capernaum); James the son of Alphaeus, and Lebbaeus, whose surname was Thaddaeus; Simon the Canaanite, and Judas Iscariot, who also betrayed him."

He calls those 12 men—11 of them will be used of God to change the course of history. One will be the betrayer. It is generally observed that Judas was the only disciple who was from Judea in the south. All the others were from Galilee. Therefore, they are sometimes referred to as Galileans or the men of Galilee.

Then the Bible says in Matthew 10:5-6 that Jesus commissioned them: *"These twelve Jesus sent forth, and commanded them, saying, Go not into the way of the Gentiles, and into any city of the Samaritans enter ye not: But go rather to the lost sheep of the house of Israel."*

Later, in John 4:1-26, Jesus will go to Samaria. He'll preach the gospel to the woman at the well. He will talk with this **Samaritan** woman who had already been married five times and is living with a man who isn't even her husband. Jesus will sit down at the well and engage her in a conversation and ask her for a drink. She will say to Him, "I am shocked. I'm a Samaritan, and you're obviously a Jew. How is it that you, being a Jew, would ask me, a Samaritan, for a drink?"

> "The very first person recorded to whom Jesus acknowledges that He is the Messiah is a woman, not a man; a Samaritin, not a Jew; and a sinner, not a saint"

Jesus will say to her, "If you knew who you are talking to you, you would be asking Me for a drink of living water so that you'd never thirst again." He will get her attention. She will ask for that water because He will trigger her curiously, but ultimately, He wants to convert her soul.

Eventually, they will start talking about whether a person should worship God in Jerusalem or in the mountains of Samaria. Jesus will tell her clearly in that passage in John 4 that salvation is of the Jews, but nevertheless, God is not seeking people to worship Him in a place, whether it's Jerusalem or Samaria. Instead, we are to worship Him in the heart, in spirit, and in truth.

Then, in verses 25-26, it says, *"The woman saith unto him, I know that Messias cometh, which is called Christ: when he is come, he will tell us all things* (he will speak the truth). *Jesus saith unto her, I that speak unto thee am he."* The very first person recorded (that we know of) to whom Jesus acknowledges that He is the Messiah is a woman, not a man; a Samaritan, not a Jew; and a sinner, not a saint. This is because Jesus wants to make it clear that He has come to be the Savior of all men—of Jews and Gentiles alike.

In Matthew 28 in His Great Commission after the resurrection, Jesus will tell the disciples to go into all the world and preach the Gospel to all nations, but at this early point of His ministry, Jesus clearly focuses the ministry on the people of Israel.

He's challenging the disciples: "You go out. You preach the message of the Gospel and tell people that the kingdom of God is available to them if they will receive it in their hearts. Tell them, God can save your soul, change your life, and even heal your body. God can do miracles on your behalf."

Jesus gives the disciples the power to do this, as well. It's unique to the apostles. They have apostolic authority to do the miraculous and to receive a direct revelation from God.

Later, they will write the Word of God. They will record for us the very words of Jesus that are inspired of God. In the meantime, Jesus wants the disciples to go to the house of Israel because Jesus has come, first and foremost, to make Himself available as the promised Messiah of Israel.

Jesus is clearly saying, just as He said to the woman at the well, "I am the Messiah," which is the *Mashiach* or, in the Greek translation, the *Christos* for the Christ. So, when we say the name Jesus Christ, we're really saying Jesus the Christ or Jesus the Messiah. We are recognizing the fact that Jesus is the promised Messiah from the Old Testament.

In Genesis 3:15, He is the One who would be born of a woman and would enter the human race in order to meet our need and crush the head of the serpent—Satan. He is the One who is born of the virgin in Isaiah 7:14. He is the One who is the mighty God in Isaiah 9:6. That passage also tells us that He's the Prince of Peace, Wonderful, Counsellor, and mighty God. It also tells us that the government will be on His shoulders.

Ultimately, He's born to be a **King**. Jesus will say to Pilate in John 18:36 that it is unto this end that He was born—to be a King—but that His kingdom is a spiritual kingdom.

You see, the kingdom that Jesus is going to launch is a kingdom of the heart. He didn't come to overthrow the Roman government, even though many of the Jewish people had hoped that the Messiah would do exactly that. He hadn't even come to overthrow the Jewish system. He makes it clear in Matthew 5:17 that He didn't come to destroy the Law, but to fulfill the Law. In Him, all the Law will come to its ultimate fulfillment. Jesus wants people to understand the spiritual nature of the Law in His teachings.

The message of Jesus is a message that goes beyond the Law of the Old Testament. It goes beyond the rituals, the routines, and even the sacrifices of the Old Testament system. It's a message that says God wants to change your heart. God wants to have a relationship with you personally. Yes, God does care how

Sunrise on the Sea of Galilee

you live and what you do with your hands. God does care what we think in our minds. And God does want to inflame the passion of our hearts. However, until your heart is born by the power of God and until your mind fully understands the claims of Christ, only then can you realize what He meant when He said, "Come, follow Me."

Everyone who has to face that claim has to ask himself, "Am I really willing to be His disciple? Am I really willing to be one who is a learner under the authority of the Master?" It is only much later many years after the death of Christ that His followers become known as Christians—Christ ones. Why? It's because His followers of the Way had been so successful at being learners and disciples that they finally deserved to be called Christians.

We sometimes tend to reverse that process and tell a new believer, "Now you are a Christian." They are, but you need to be a disciple. The Biblical model is that you need to learn to be Christ's disciple so that, when you claim to be a Christ one, it will be obvious to everybody that Jesus Christ lives within your heart and life and that He's changed your thinking. Because of this change, He's inflamed your heart, and He's using your hands, so to speak, to touch the world for the cause of Christ.

There are many challenges in the world in which we live, but all of us need to take a quiet moment of reflection and ask ourselves, "Is Jesus really who He said He is? Is He really the promised Messiah?"

There are over 100 prophesies about the **Messiah** in the Old Testament. Jesus fulfilled every single one of them to the glory of God.

Not one of the chosen 12 disciples was a scholar or a rabbi. They were, for the most part, fishermen and tradesmen. Yet, Jesus would call them the light of the world, a title often bequeathed on scholars and on leading rabbis. These men are the students of Jesus.

Jesus will devote the majority of His time over the next three years preparing these ordinary men to do extraordinary things. They will be transformed by the teaching of Jesus, and they in turn will become teachers and leaders of the early church. They will proclaim that Jesus is the Messiah predicted by the prophets, and they will remain steadfast in their mission to build the church even under severe persecution. Their decision to follow Jesus will cost them their families, their fortunes, and their very lives. Nearly all of the disciples will be martyred for their devotion to Jesus.

Being a **disciple** of Jesus is not easy. Jesus warned His initial disciples in Matthew 10:16, *"Behold, I send you forth as sheep in the midst of wolves: be ye therefore wise as serpents, and harmless as doves."* Being a Christian and sharing your faith means being intentional about sharing your faith. God wants to use your mouth, as well as the example of your life. However, He wants us to use wisdom and tact in how we share the Gospel powerfully and effectively with others.

Then, He told the disciples not everybody is going to believe. Not everybody is going to respond. If they've rejected Me, they will reject you. If they think I'm empowered by the devil because I can cast out the devil, what do you think they will think of you?

None of us should be surprised when believers are made fun of and castigated in some way in the public media. We ought to expect that. Now, we ought to be cautious not to cause that to happen because of our own foolishness. As you share the message of Christ clearly and directly with people, know that, when you decide, you divide.

Jesus made that very, very clear to the disciples. In Matthew 10:32-33 and 38, He said, *"Whosoever therefore shall confess me before men, him will I confess also before my Father which is in heaven. But whosoever shall deny me before men, him will I also deny before my Father which is in heaven… And he that taketh not his cross, and followeth after me, is not worthy of me."*

Now, when you think about the person of Jesus Christ, think about your own personal life. Ask yourself, "Am I a secret believer or a closet Christian?" Well, Jesus doesn't need any more secret disciples. He doesn't need any more secret agents sleuthing around unidentified throughout the world. They only flash their Christian paraphernalia when they see another believer, and it's like, "Hi, Christian buddy. Don't tell anybody we're here." Jesus doesn't need that from us.

He needs believers who are real disciples, who have a passion for Him, and who have a radical faith, but who are also wise, cautious, humble, and effective in how they share that faith. They do it to the glory of God. God wants to use you as a spiritual soldier in the battle against the forces of evil and injustice in our own day and age.

Just as Jesus called His disciples from the shores of the Sea of Galilee, He wants to call you into His service as well, but not everybody's going to love what you have to say. Many will, but some will not. Be prepared to face rejection. Be prepared to face animosity, if necessary.

I think it's also important for us to understand that the **real issue** is the response of the person to whom we speak. If they confess Jesus before men, He will confess them before the Father, but if they deny Christ before men, are they a Christian? Some might respond, "Well, I don't know. Maybe. What do you mean?" That's a denial. That's what Peter ended up doing the night that he denied the Lord. Then, pretty soon, it was, "No, I don't really know Him." The denial got more severe and direct. That might not be you. Perhaps you're

still struggling with the claims of Christ and asking yourself, "Is He really who He says He is? Can He really do what He says He can do? Can He change my life and save my soul. Am I willing to confess Him before men?

The Scripture tells us in Romans 10:9, *"That if thou shalt confess with thy mouth the Lord Jesus, and shalt believe in thine heart that God hath raised him from the dead, thou shalt be saved."* That's the power of Jesus' message that we call the Gospel. The Good News of salvation is that the Son of God took your sin upon Himself. He died in your place and bore the wrath of God against sin. He rose from the dead triumphantly to offer you and me the gift of eternal life.

When a person trusts Jesus as their Savior, they are not merely saying, "Oh, I believe that Jesus lived," or "I believe He was a great teacher and good person." It's far more than that. It is saying, "I believe that He is who He says He is—the sinless Son of God who went to the cross to take my place and die for my sins. I'm putting my faith and trust in what He did on the cross. I'm saying that's enough, and I believe it. I receive it by the grace of God; I express it by the faith of my heart and life. I embrace it with confidence and commitment and say yes to Him."

If you've never done that, understand that it's not about the words you say, but it's

really about having the right heart attitude. However, you might pray something like the following in your own words:

Dear God, I realize that I have failed you many times. I've fallen far short of your glory—that's for sure. But, right now, I do believe that Jesus died for me and that He rose from the dead for me. I'm putting my faith and trust in Him. I'm trusting that invitation of the Bible that, 'Whoever calls upon the name of the Lord will be saved.' Save me right now, Jesus, and change me right now.

Pray that in Jesus' name. Pray it with a confidence of an "Amen." God will hear you, and God will answer your prayer.

CHAPTER 5
SERMON ON THE MOUNT

Location: Region of Galilee, Circa A.D. 30/33

"*Blessed are the poor in spirit: for theirs is the kingdom of heaven. Blessed are they that mourn: for they shall be comforted. Blessed are the meek: for they shall inherit the earth. Blessed are they which do hunger and thirst after righteousness: for they shall be filled. Blessed are the merciful: for they shall obtain mercy. Blessed are the pure in heart: for they shall see God. Blessed are the peacemakers: for they shall be called the children of God. Blessed are they which are persecuted for righteousness' sake: for theirs is the kingdom of heaven.*"

MATTHEW 5:3-10

When we listen to the Sermon on the Mount, which stunned its audience, the Bible says the people were astonished at Christ's doctrine. He taught them as One who has authority. He wasn't like the scribes and Pharisees who quoted rabbi after rabbi, as well as this opinion and that opinion. No Jesus, like the prophets of old, said, *"Thus saith the Lord."*

But the question is, what is He saying to you and me today? What foundation are you building your life on? Is it the shifting sands of human opinion and human philosophies that come and go and change with the winds of time, or are you building it on the Rock? Put your faith in the One who alone said, "I am the Way, the Truth, and the Life; follow me."

The Beatitudes

Early in His ministry, Jesus gathers His followers on a mount overlooking the Sea of Galilee. Here, Jesus will lay out what have been called the principles of the kingdom of God. He begins His teaching with a series of blessed statements known as the Beatitudes.

They were recorded in Matthew 5:3-10, which says:

Blessed are the poor in spirit: for theirs is the kingdom of heaven. Blessed are they that mourn: for they shall be comforted. Blessed are the meek: for they shall inherit the earth. Blessed are they which do hunger and thirst after righteousness: for they shall be filled. Blessed are the merciful: for they shall obtain mercy. Blessed are the pure in heart: for they shall see God. Blessed are the peacemakers: for they shall be called the children of God. Blessed are they which are persecuted for righteousness' sake: for theirs is the kingdom of heaven.

Jesus Christ has been called the greatest teacher that ever lived. There are over two billion people on earth today who claim to be His followers. These people are attracted to His teachings to His person and His power.

Of all of Jesus' teachings, perhaps the most famous is the **Sermon on the Mount**. The Gospel tells us that Jesus went about the region of Galilee preaching in the synagogues of the Jewish people. He came to preach the message, "Repent for the kingdom of heaven is at hand," but sometimes the crowds were

The Arbel Cliffs overlooking the Valley of the Doves are just some of the mountains in Galilee

so large and so overwhelming that Jesus would go outdoors, and there, along the way of life, He would find a place to preach to the people.

In Matthew 5:1-2, the Bible says, *"And seeing the multitudes, he went up into a mountain: and when he was set* (sitting down)*, his disciples came unto him: And he opened his mouth, and taught them."* So the message of the Sermon on the Mount is really a **message of discipleship** for those who are followers of Jesus Christ. It begins with the Beatitudes, the blessed statements. In the Greek text of the original Scripture, it is the word *Makarioi*, which literally means happy.

Matthew 5:3 says, *"Blessed* (or fulfilled) *are the poor in spirit: for theirs is the kingdom of heaven."* In the Greek language, there are two words for poor. *Penes* means the working poor, and *ptochos* means the desperately poor or the beggars. That's the word used here—blessed are the spiritual beggars for theirs is the kingdom of heaven. What He meant by that is we are blessed when we realize it's not about us. It's all about us receiving the gift from Him because it's all about Him.

When we come to the end of ourselves and are not full of pride, full of arrogance, full of ourselves, and full of our good works, we're the poor in spirit—the desperate. We spiritual beggars reach out for the spiritual bread, if you will, that God offers us, and we receive it by faith.

Matthew 5:4 says, *"Blessed are they that mourn: for they shall be comforted."* When you're suffering, God promises comfort.

> "As spiritual beggers, we reach out for the spiritual bread that God offers us, and we receive it by faith"

Verse 5 continues, *"Blessed are the meek: for they shall inherit the earth."* That's a passage out of the Old Testament—Psalm 37:11. Jesus has read the Old Testament, and He is applying its teaching to His disciples.

Verse 6 says, *"Blessed are they which do hunger and thirst after righteousness: for they shall be filled."* He didn't say blessed are those that are hungry physically, but instead, He said, *"Blessed are they which do hunger and thirst after righteousness."* God will fulfill the need in their lives.

Then, He says in Verse 7, *"Blessed are the merciful: for they shall obtain mercy."* In other words, if you show mercy, you'll receive mercy.

Verse 8 states, *"Blessed are the pure in heart: for they shall see God."* Now, in reality, none of us is really pure in heart in and of ourselves. That takes the spiritual transformation that occurs when you're born by the Spirit of God. God creates a purity in our hearts that comes from Him and not from us.

Next, in Verse 9, Jesus says, *"Blessed are the peacemakers: for they shall be called the children of God."* Real followers of Jesus Christ are those who have made peace with God and who have experienced the peace of God in their hearts and souls. Therefore, we ought to be able to express peacefulness in our relationship with one another. That's why he will later not only say, "Love your neighbor as yourself," but also, "Love your enemy." As a peacemaker, we have not come to create controversy, but to bring peace.

Then, He says in Verse 10, *"Blessed are they which are persecuted for righteousness' sake: for theirs is the kingdom of heaven."* When we've done everything right that we know to do in order to serve the Lord and yet we suffer rejection, persecution, or humiliation because of righteousness, He says you are blessed. What He's trying to help us

The traditional site of the Sermon
on the Mount marked by a Basilica
run by the Catholic church

understand is that, in the worst situations of the human experience, you are truly fully blessed if you're at peace with God and if God is at work in your heart and life.

In fact, in Verse 11, He goes on to say, *"Blessed are ye, when men shall revile you, and persecute you, and shall say all manner of evil against you falsely,"* notice, *"for my sake."* This is not because of some foolish thing we did, but for standing up for Christ and the cause of righteousness.

Verse 12 says, *"Rejoice, and be exceeding glad: for great is your reward in heaven."* The beatitudes are the blessings of happiness—the "be right" attitudes, if you will. When you and I have the right attitude toward the problems and pressures of life, it's because the Spirit of God is at work in our lives to enable us to live like Jesus intended for us to live.

Intensive Discipleship

Jesus has gathered His closest followers on a mountainside overlooking the Sea of Galilee. For Matthew, Simon, James, John, and others who have become part of Jesus' inner circle, this is a time of intensive discipleship. These men are now the students of Jesus. They will become witness to His miracles and witness to His message to humanity. These ordinary men will be transformed by the teaching of Jesus. They will become teachers and leaders

of the early church. They will learn that they can do extraordinary things by the grace and power of God.

The beatitudes are followed by Jesus' statement that His disciples are the salt of the earth and the light of the world. In other words, He is telling them that, if you're going to live out your Christianity in this fallen world, you need to live as salt that preserves, convicts, and even melts the ice of the human heart. You need to live as the light that shines into the darkness. No matter how dark it is, the smallest light, the tiniest candle, or the littlest flashlight will begin to light up the darkness. If enough believers show the life of Christ as the light of the world, then we begin to make a difference in this dark and fallen place.

Then, in Matthew 5:17, Jesus said, *"Think not that I am come to destroy the law, or the prophets: I am not come to destroy, but to fulfil."* I'm sure the disciples were wondering, "Are you contradicting Moses?" Jesus' answer is, "No, I have come to fulfill the intent of what Moses said. I have not come to destroy it."

In fact, in the English version, Verse 18 says, *"Till heaven and earth pass, one jot or one tittle shall in no wise pass from the law, till all be fulfilled."* A jot is the *Yodh*, which is the smallest letter of the Hebrew alphabet, and the tittle is the smallest piece of the letter. A tiddle is the difference in Hebrew between an 'r' and a 'd.' Jesus said, "I want you to know not one of these will pass until all of the Scripture is fulfilled."

Whoever breaks any of the commandments is guilty of breaking all of them. Now, that's the problem. Sometimes in our humanness, we have the tendency to think, "Well, I'm as good as the next guy," or "I'm not as bad as that person." Yet, the Bible reminds us in

passages such as James 2:10 that, if we have sinned at all, we are guilty of being sinners. Therefore, we fall short of the standard of God's righteousness.

While people often go about with good works trying to earn their way to heaven, the Bible makes it clear that our good works don't produce our salvation. They are the **fruit** of our

> ## Our good works will never produce salvation; they are only the fruit of our salvation

salvation. They're the evidence that God is at work in our lives through faith in the message of the Gospel (See Ephesians 2:8-10).

Then, Jesus gives a series of contrasts from the Old Testament to what will become the New Testament. He says in Matthew 5:21-22, *"Ye have heard that it was said by them of old time"*—in other words, this is the ancient tradition—*"Thou shalt not kill; and whosoever shall kill shall be in danger of the judgment. But I say unto you, That whosoever is angry with his brother without a cause shall be in danger of the judgment."* Being angry at someone without cause is a sin just like murder.

Verses 27-28 say, *"Thou shalt not commit adultery: But I say unto you, That whosoever looketh on a woman to lust after her hath committed adultery with her already in his heart."* You have virtually committed adultery with her already in your mind.

In reference to divorce, perhaps your attitude is, "I'm going to put away my wife and give her a bill of divorcement," which was allowed in the Law of Moses. However, while Moses permitted divorce, he did not promote it. Jesus says here in Matthew 5:32-33, *"But I say unto you, That whosoever shall put away his wife, **saving for the cause of fornication**, causeth her to commit adultery: and whosoever shall marry her that is divorced committeth adultery."* In other words, don't divorce your wife at all except for the cause of adultery or fornication. Don't look for a way to get out of your marriage commitment.

If you really know God and if God is at work in your life, you ought to want to live your life to the glory of God. That means that we are to follow the commands of God, such as husbands love your wives even as Christ loved the church and love your neighbor as yourself. Your wife is your closest neighbor, your dwelling mate. Well, you say, "I don't get along at all with my wife." Then, love your enemies to the glory of God (Matthew 5:44).

You see, God never lets us off the hook. We've got to learn to love everybody. If He expects you to love your enemy and love your neighbor, He surely expects you to love your spouse—your husband or your wife.

Jesus then said in Matthew 5:33-37, *"Again, ye have heard that it hath been said by them of old time, Thou shalt not forswear thyself, but shalt perform unto the Lord thine oaths: But I say unto you, Swear not at all; neither by heaven; for it is God's throne: Nor by the earth; for it is his footstool: neither by Jerusalem; for it is the city of the great King. Neither shalt thou swear by thy head, because thou canst not make one hair white or black. But let your communication be, Yea, yea; Nay, nay."* This is saying, if you make a vow unto the Lord, make sure you perform it. Don't break the vow. In fact, don't make any vows. Too often, people make vows that they really do not intend to keep. Let your yes be yes and your no be no. Speak the truth; say the truth; live the truth; and do the truth.

Living Out God's Principles

Having laid out His principles in Chapter 5, Jesus then begins to apply them practically to the life of his disciples. Look in your Bible in Matthew 6. Jesus gives a series of applications of what to do when you're giving your money, when you pray, and when you're fasting, and what to do with your treasures and possessions. Who really are you ultimately serving?

Religious activity is something all of us value if we are believers. I need to pray. I need to give. I need to show some discipline. I even need to learn to fast and deny myself food or some other special indulgence of some sort. Yet, Jesus makes it clear that those customary activities of religiosity don't always reveal a heart for God.

In Matthew 6:1, He says, *"Take heed that ye do not your alms before men* (give money to the poor), *to be seen of them: otherwise ye have no reward of your Father which is in heaven."* In other words, when you're giving money to the Lord's work, which we all ought to do, don't do it for show. Verses 2 and 3 tell us why we should not insist they put your name on a plaque in front of the stained glass window or put your name on the seat in the church or on some hall that is dedicated to you. Jesus is saying to give your gifts in secret. Then, Verse 4 explains, *"Thy Father which seeth in secret himself shall reward thee openly."*

In Verse 5, Jesus tells the disciples, *"And when thou prayest, thou shalt not be as the hypocrites are: for they love to pray standing in the synagogues and in the corners of the streets, that they may be seen of men."* Now, that does not mean that God is against public prayer. You have plenty of examples of public prayers in the Book of Acts. In Acts, we see believers who are gathered together in prayer meetings. They are praying for the apostles to be released from prison, for healing of an individual, for a blessing, or for a miracle from God. Collective prayer is part of the life of the church. His point is, don't use your praying to show off to people. Use it to talk to God.

In other words, what we are on our knees before God is what we really are, not what we say when we pray in public. We still ought to pray publically. I think asking a blessing over a meal is a wonderful thing to do. Jesus did it. He blessed the bread, broke it, and distributed it to the disciples. It's a very typical Jewish thing to do. It's also a very important Christian thing to do.

Just because we bow our heads and say a few words doesn't mean we really prayed. Some people will sit down in a restaurant, do a quick dip with their head, and then sit right back up again in a matter of two seconds. They could not have said much more than, "Thanks." Prayer needs to come from your heart unto the Lord. You ought to cry out to God and be on your knees before the Lord in private, as well as in public.

Then, Jesus gave them an example of how to pray in Verses 9 to 13, *"After this manner therefore pray ye."* Some have called it the **Lord's prayer** because Jesus taught it, but He really taught it to the disciples. It's really their prayer. It says, *"Our Father which art in heaven, Hallowed be thy name."* He begins by addressing the prayer to God.

"Thy kingdom come. Thy will be done in earth, as it is in heaven." The will of God is done in heaven. Our desire is to see the will of God done on earth as well. We're praying

The traditional path to place of Sermon on the Mount

for His Kingdom to come because it still has not fully come. It comes into the hearts of all those who become citizens of the Kingdom by faith. However, the Kingdom in which Jesus will reign and rule on earth is yet to come at the time of the Second Coming.

Then, Jesus says, *"Give us this day our daily bread."* That's all He asks for; there are not a lot of requests here. We are just to ask Him to meet our essential needs.

"And forgive us our debts, as we forgive our debtors." Another way of saying this is to forgive those who have sinned against us. Forgive us as we are willing to forgive others.

In fact, He will go on later to say that if we do not forgive men from our heart, our Father will not really forgive us. Those who have been forgiven need to be forgiving towards others.

Then, Jesus adds, *"And lead us not into temptation, but deliver us from evil: For thine is the kingdom, and the power, and the glory, for ever. Amen."*

Back in Matthew 6:7, Jesus tells His disciples not to simply pray with vain repetitions. Now, I don't think there's anything wrong with praying the Lord's Prayer verbatim, as it's recorded in the Bible. Christians have done that for 2,000 years, but it's not as if

saying these words is magical in some sense. It's not enough to memorize the prayer. Prayer needs to come from the heart. Prayer needs to come in secret before God where we cry out to the Lord from our deepest needs.

In Verses 16 and 17, Jesus said. *"Moreover when ye fast, be not, as the hypocrites, of a sad countenance: for they disfigure their faces, that they may appear unto men to fast. Verily I say unto you, They have their reward. But thou, when thou fastest, anoint thine head, and wash thy face."* Jesus is saying that you need to change your clothes and not walk around with a sour face like, "Oh, brother! I'm fasting. Isn't that wonderful?" No, Jesus says to do it in secret unto the Lord. It's not a problem if somebody figures out that your fasting. His point is, don't go around broadcasting it as though you are telling people how spiritual you are. Just do it unto the Lord, and the Father who sees you in secret will reward you openly.

How we pray, how we give, how we fast, and how we discipline ourselves with real **spiritual disciplines** ultimately must be done unto the Lord. It's not saying, "Look at how spiritual I am." I am to do it unto God because I love Him, because I'm worshipping Him, and because I'm serving Him.

Then, Jesus says in Verses 19 and 20, *"Lay not up for yourselves treasures upon earth ... But lay up for yourselves treasures in heaven."* In other words, you cannot serve two masters (Verse 24). You either serve God or materialism. He doesn't say that material things are wrong. He's saying that can't be the priority of your heart and life. If you're living for your stuff, your stuff is not going to love you back. Ultimately, your stuff is going to let you down. It will disappoint you because life

> ## With prayer, we are to cry out to the Lord from our deepest needs

is not about the stuff that you have. It's about the God who has your heart.

In Verses 27 and 28, this is the point in the passage where Jesus tells us to consider the lilies of the field that are are clothed even greater than Solomon. Verse 26 tells us that our Father feeds the birds of the air everyday. Will He not take care of you? Aren't you much more valuable than they are? Now, that's not to say that God doesn't care about plants and animals. His point is that plants and animals are not created in the image and likeness of God—you are. If God the Creator is willing to bless His creation, is He not willing to bless you? I think Jesus wants us to understand that we don't have to be afraid of God. You don't have to run away from God. Don't have to have the attitude, "If I ever surrender my life to Christ, there's no telling what He's liable to demand that I do."

Yes, He's going to call you to take up your cross and follow Him. He's going to call you to give your life to serve Him, but in that, you'll find the greatest joy of life! God will care for you. That's the whole point of the sermon. That's why He says in Verse 33, *"But seek ye first the kingdom of God, and his righteousness; and all these things shall be added unto you."* Don't live for things. God will take care of the things that you need in life.

A Moment of Commitment

I grew up in a very ordinary lower-end, middle-class home in Detroit, Michigan. My parents dropped out of school in the eighth grade. Neither of them finished high school. Nobody in our family went to college. Nobody ever went into the ministry. In fact, nobody knew the Lord. In our home, there was no God, no Jesus, and no Bible at all.

I came to know Christ as my Savior during a Vacation Bible School at a church in our neighborhood. My mother didn't even take me. She just said, "Go there. This would be good for you to get out of the house." While I was there, I learned that Jesus loves me, that He died for my sins, that He rose from the dead, that He was coming again, that I could have my sins forgiven, and that I could have a home in heaven forever. And it was all free. I raised my hand and said, "I'm in." This was the best deal I had ever heard of.

In Matthew 7, Jesus brings the entire message down to a moment of commitment for His listeners. He says in Matthew 7:13-14, *"Enter ye in at the strait gate: for wide is the gate, and broad is the way, that leadeth to destruction, and many there be which go in thereat: Because strait is the gate, and narrow is the way, which leadeth unto life, and few there be that find it."* This is perhaps one of the most convicting statements in all of this message.

Then, He says in Verses 15 and 16, *"Beware of false prophets, which come to you in sheep's clothing, but inwardly they are ravening wolves. Ye shall know them by their fruits."* He doesn't tell us to go around judging everybody else. In fact, in Verse 1 of this chapter, it says, *"Judge not, that ye be not judged."* There's a difference between being judgmental about somebody else's behavior and being wise and showing spiritual discernment. Here, He balances the judge not statement in the first part of the chapter with His statement that by their fruits you will know them.

In Verses 16 and 17, we continue to read, *"Do men gather grapes of thorns, or figs of thistles? Even so every good tree bringeth forth good fruit; but a corrupt tree bringeth forth evil fruit."* Jesus' theme always is that, in the life of a real believer, there will be some fruit. No fruit means no life. No salvation means no transformation. Even if a person claims to be a believer, if their life does not show any evidence of that, don't trust that profession. It may be false.

Verse 21 says, *"Not every one that saith unto me, Lord, Lord, shall enter into the kingdom of heaven; but he that doeth the will of my Father which is in heaven."* Then, Verse 23 says, *"And then will I profess unto them, I never knew you: depart from me."* You professed in my name. You said that you tried to live by My teaching, but I never knew you. I never came to live within your heart and life. I never changed you, and you know that. You are still the same old person you always were and are still struggling with the same old issues you have always struggled with. This is because your pride keeps resisting the power of the penetration of the real Gospel message that will change and transform you forever.

Jesus then ends the message saying, *"I will liken him unto a wise man, which built his house upon a rock: And the rain descended, and the floods came, and the winds blew,*

and beat upon that house; and it fell not: for it was founded upon a rock. And every one that heareth these sayings of mine, and doeth them not, shall be likened unto a foolish man, which built his house upon the sand. And the rain descended, and the floods came, and the winds blew, and beat upon that house; and it fell: and great was the fall of it."

In other words, what **foundation** are you going to build your life on? Will it be upon the shifting sands of human opinion and human philosophies that ultimately have ended up concluding there is no meaning or purpose to life? If so, then life is just a matter of random existence with no sense of real direction, fulfillment, purpose or accomplishment at all. You are just a speck of protoplasm on a biological horizon of millions of years of humanity, and then you are out of here and gone.

Or is it true that you're created in the image and likeness of God to have a relationship with God? Is it true that Jesus came not just to teach us the way, but also to show us the way to live the life? Yes, He came to give His life so that you and I might experience the life of God and so that…

we might become the salt of the earth and the light of the world!

Approximately 90% of the Gospel narrative happened within the pictured geological area of the region of Galilee as seen from the Arbel Overlook

◄ Bethsaida

◄ Sermon on
the Mount

◄ Chorazin

◄ Capernaum

Jesus Calls ▼
James & John

CHAPTER 6
HIS PARABLES

Location: Region of Galilee, Circa A.D. 30/33

"*Therefore speak I to them in parables: because they seeing see not; and hearing they hear not, neither do they understand. And in them is fulfilled the prophecy of Esaias, which saith, By hearing ye shall hear, and shall not understand; and seeing ye shall see, and shall not perceive: For this people's heart is waxed gross, and their ears are dull of hearing, and their eyes they have closed; lest at any time they should see with their eyes, and hear with their ears, and should understand with their heart, and should be converted, and I should heal them.*"

MATTHEW 13:13-15

The teachings of Jesus are among the most famous in all of history. Jesus is especially known for His ability to tell parables. A parable is an illustration, if you will. Some have called it an earthly story with a heavenly meaning. In other words, it's a story about everyday life that the people of Jesus' time would have clearly understood, but the story illustrates a spiritual or eternal truth.

It is early in the first century, and a young Jewish Carpenter and itinerant Preacher from Nazareth is making His way to the great freshwater lake known as the Sea of Galilee. Here in the northern part of Israel far from Jerusalem, He will make the startling claim that the Kingdom of God is at hand.

He will present Himself not as a political figure, nor as a revolutionary. He will instead appear to be a humble rabbi or teacher. Yet, He is unlike any rabbi the people of Galilee have ever seen.

This Rabbi eats with tax collectors and sinners. He has even gone as far to spare a local prostitute from punishment. He has

Dr. Hindson in the synagogue at Chorazin in Galilee standing near the decoration by the synagogue scroll ark

also, according to religious authorities, marginalized or even violated the Sabbath rules outright. But, when He speaks, Jesus says amazing things. He has such a command of the Scriptures. He does not speak from scholarly commentary, but directly from the written Word of God.

Jesus quickly becomes a sensation among the people of Galilee. His fame is, no doubt, driven by the supernatural things that happen whenever He is around. Witnesses will say that, when Jesus speaks, miracles occur and demons flee.

By all accounts, Jesus is a **compelling personality**. He has a way of teaching from Scripture that is relatable to the common man. He is credited with a teaching technique known as a parable. It is a kind of moral storytelling used to illustrate a Biblical truth. Gospel writers will record no less than 46 such moral stories as Jesus teaches in the towns and villages in the region of Galilee. When asked by His disciples why Jesus taught in this manner, He replied in Matthew 13:13-15:

Therefore speak I to them in parables: because they seeing see not; and

JESUS OF THE BIBLE

The Seeds
of Israel

hearing they hear not, neither do they understand. And in them is fulfilled the prophecy of Esaias, which saith, By hearing ye shall hear, and shall not understand; and seeing ye shall see, and shall not perceive: For this people's heart is waxed gross, and their ears are dull of hearing, and their eyes they have closed; lest at any time they should see with their eyes, and hear with their ears, and should understand with their heart, and should be converted, and I should heal them.

The Parable of the Sower

One of Jesus' most famous stories is the "Parable of the Sower." A sower goes forth in the field to sow the seed, to plant a crop, to deliver the fruit of the crop, to feed his family or perhaps to sell to others.

In Matthew 13:4-8, Jesus says, *"And when he sowed, some seeds fell by the way side* (on the road), *and the fowls came and devoured them up: Some fell upon stony places, where they had not much earth: and forthwith they sprung up, because they had no deepness of earth: And when the sun was up, they were scorched; and because they had no root, they withered away. And some fell among thorns; and the thorns sprung up, and choked them:*

But other fell into good ground, and brought forth fruit, some an hundredfold, some sixtyfold, some thirtyfold."

He sows the seed in four different types of ground—he sows some seeds by the wayside along the road, some in stony places where there wasn't much earth, some among the thorns, and some in the good ground. Each one of these illustrates a different response of the human heart.

> *A parable is designed to help the listener understand the point Jesus is making*

Jesus goes on to explain each one of the **four types of ground**. With the seed that falls on the road or wayside, the fowls or birds come and devour the seed. It is like the seed is lying on a road, and it cannot take root or germinate in any way at all. Eventually, the birds come along and devour the seed.

With the second type, Jesus says that the seeds fall among the stony places where there isn't much earth (ground). The plant then takes a short, narrow route and springs up

quickly, but ultimately, it is burned away by the sun and withers away because it doesn't have a proper root.

The third type is where the seeds fall among thorns. A plant starts to grow, but eventually, the thorns choke it out.

The fourth example is the only one where the seeds fall on good ground. That ground is well plowed and well prepared, and the seed takes root. It brought forth fruit. In all four of these distinctions, only this one brings forth fruit; the others do not.

A parable is normally used to illustrate a point. It is designed to help the listener understand the point that Jesus is making. However, in the case of the "Parable of the Sower," the disciples aren't even sure what it means, so Jesus interprets it for them.

Rather than wild-eyed speculation trying to understand the meaning of a parable, we need to compare Scripture with Scripture. We need to look at other parts of the Bible and, in this case, at Jesus' own explanation of what it means.

In Matthew 13:18-19, Jesus says of the first, *"Hear ye therefore the parable of the sower. When any one heareth the word of the kingdom, and understandeth it not, then cometh the wicked one, and catcheth away that which was sown in his heart. This is* he which received seed by the way side." In other words, as the message of the Gospel of the Good News of Jesus goes forth, there are some people who make no response at all. This is the **hardhearted** response, where the seed does not have any root. There is no response, and Satan steals away even that seed that they've heard.

Of the second, Jesus says in Verses 20 and 21, *"But he that received the seed into stony places, the same is he that heareth the word, and anon with joy receiveth it; Yet hath he not root in himself, but dureth for a while: for when tribulation or persecution ariseth because of the word, by and by he is offended."* This example is like a person who receives the Word and is filled with joy and excitement when he receives it. However, he has no root, and therefore, he does not endure. When tribulation or persecution arises from the world, he gets offended and is gone. In other words, there has been no real saving faith—no real lasting faith. It doesn't change the individual's life.

There are people who go to a meeting and hear a message. They get all excited and even attempt to make some kind of a response, but the response is only **emotional**. They may be excited about what they think Jesus can do for them, but it's not a commitment of their heart and life to Him. They do not commit to the person of Christ to really be His disciple and follower.

Then, Jesus says of the third one in Verse 22, *"He also that received seed among the thorns is he that heareth the word; and the care of this world, and the deceitfulness of riches, choke the word, and he becometh unfruitful."* The person who receives this seed is among the thorns. He hears the Word, but the cares of this world and deceitfullness of riches choke out the Word. In other words, this is the **worldly** response from a person who is so caught up in the things of the world that he really doesn't respond to the things of Christ.

Now, look at Verse 23, *"But he that received seed into the good ground is he that heareth the word, and understandeth it; which also beareth fruit, and bringeth forth, some an hundredfold, some sixty, some thirty."* Jesus says the seed that falls on the good ground takes root and produces fruit. This is the person who hears the Word and **understands** it. The response to the Gospel is intellectual, as well as spiritual, as well as emotional.

You have to understand that Jesus' death on the cross is an atonement for your sins and that on the cross He takes the wrath of God against our sin. He dies in our place. He rises on our behalf. If I don't understand that, I'm going to spend my entire lifetime trying to make God happy, trying to work my way to heaven, and trying to please God in some way with all the good things that I've done. Yet, the Bible tells us in Isaiah 64:6, *"All our righteousnesses* (good works) *are as filthy rags,"* in the sight of God. You can never work your way to heaven. The "Good News," though, is God has worked His way to you.

Notice what He says about the person who receives the Word, hears the Word, and understands the Word. He says, *"...which also beareth fruit, and bringeth forth, some an hundredfold, some sixty, some thirty."* In other words, the amount of **spiritual fruit** that might be produced in a believer's life may vary from one person to another. Some will produce fruit a hundred fold, some only thirty, some only sixty, but Jesus gave no true believer the option of producing no fruit.

No fruit means no life. It also means no spiritual transformation at all. Good people differ on how to interpret that parable. Some see the response of the shallow ground or the thorny ground as people who make a commitment of faith to Christ and later fall away. Others say, no, it's obvious in the passage the only true believer is the fourth one. Only he hears the Word and understands it so that it takes root in his heart and life and produces real fruit. I personally think that's the correct understanding of that parable.

Jesus is reminding us that, when people make no response at all, don't expect to see any fruit in their life. They've said no to the One who alone can change their life.

The Parable of the Wheat & the Tares

Jesus also tells the "Parable of the Wheat and the Tares." It is about a farmer who goes out to sow wheat in his field expecting to reap a crop from which he could make bread. In the meantime, his enemy comes along and sows tares among the wheat.

From the top surface view, the two look alike when they first spring up. You can't tell the difference between them. The question is, should we rip the tares out from among the wheat? The response of the farmer is no, don't do that. If you try to pull out every single weed, you will pull out the wheat in the process. In other words, you'll damage the crop.

Then, Jesus explained the parable. The wheat represents the believers, but among the true believers, there will always be some tares. There will always be some weeds. These people may profess faith in Christ and may look or act like a believer, but in reality,

Dr. Hindson holds both wheat and a tare in his hand

they really are not. How do we know that? Again, it's because there is no fruit.

On the question of the tare, the challenge that we often face in life is to determine, "Am I wheat, or am I a tare? Do I just look like a Christian and act like a Christian, but not really have a heart for God and the things of God? Or, is my life spiritually fruitful, like the wheat? Am I producing real evidence of my salvation? Can God use the testimony of my life to speak to others?"

You see, God is not concerned so much about whether or not there are tares or false professions among the members of your church. There are always going to be people like that. People are always going to disappoint you. Even some preachers are going to disappoint you.

Ultimately, God is looking for people who have a heart for Him. The evidence of their real salvation is the fruitfulness of their experience with God Himself.

The "Lost" Parables

Jesus is traveling throughout the region of Galilee speaking in public places and teaching in the synagogues. Wherever He goes, Jesus draws large crowds anxious to hear His message of healing and hope. He will travel from town to town with just the clothes on His back. He will rely on the kindness of strangers for provision of food and shelter.

Jesus' journeys take Him into the places of the righteous and the unrighteous. His followers will soon learn that Jesus does not separate Himself from those of ill repute. His message of forgiveness and His friendship are extended to all, even to those whom society would shun. Jesus demonstrates by Word and action that He is willing to engage the sick, the poor, and the sinner.

Central to His message is the idea of God as a Heavenly Father who desires the spiritual restoration of His people. Jesus describes those who are apart from God and His Word as "lost." He will evoke images of lostness in three parables, as He speaks about the lost sheep, the lost coin, and the lost son.

> *Jesus describes those who are apart from God and His Word as 'lost'*

Of all of Jesus' parables, the parable of "The Prodigal Son" is one of the most familiar. In Luke 15, Luke opens the chapter by saying that the Pharisees are objecting to the fact that Jesus is ministering to sinners and that He is even eating with them. Jesus has to explain to them that God didn't send Him to be a physician to the healthy, but to the sick. Luke 19:10 says, *"For the Son of man is come to seek and to save that which was lost."* He hasn't come to seek the saved. He has come to seek the lost. We always see the evangelistic heart of God reaching out to recover the lost.

There are three lost things in this chapter. The chapter opens with the first illustration in the parable of **"The Lost Sheep."** Jesus said in Luke 15:4-7, *"What man of you, having an hundred sheep, if he lose one of them, doth not leave the ninety and nine in the wilderness, and go after that which is lost, until he find it? And when he hath found it, he layeth it on his shoulders, rejoicing. And when he cometh* *home, he calleth together his friends and neighbours, saying unto them, Rejoice with me; for I have found my sheep which was lost. I say unto you, that likewise joy shall be in heaven over one sinner that repenteth, more than over ninety and nine just persons, which need no repentance."*

If there's a shepherd who has 100 sheep and loses one of them, he will leave the 99 safe in the fold and go seek the one sheep that is lost. When he finds it, he'll put it on his shoulders and carry it back to the sheepfold. He will rejoice because that which was lost has been found. Then Jesus said, *"...likewise joy shall be in heaven over one sinner that repenteth, more than over ninety and nine just persons, which need no repentance."*

The second illustration is the parable of the woman with **"The Lost Coin"** found in Luke 15:8-10, *"Either what woman having ten pieces of silver, if she lose one piece, doth not light a candle, and sweep the house, and seek diligently till she find it? And when she hath found it, she calleth her friends and her neighbours together, saying, Rejoice with me; for I have found the piece which I had lost. Likewise, I say unto you, there is joy in the presence of the angels of God over one sinner that repenteth."*

The woman has 10 pieces of silver. Some have suggested that women often wore coins

as part of the jewelry, part of their bridal price. This jewelry was an indication that she was a married woman, a blessed woman. So losing one of those pieces is more than just losing an ordinary coin. Therefore, she searches the house diligently looking for the lost coin. When she finds it, she rejoices and calls all of her friends together to celebrate with her.

Jesus is using this story to prepare the audience for what is coming in the parable of "The Prodigal Son."

In the third "lost" illustration or parable, Jesus tells the story of "**The Lost Son**," which is known to many as the parable of "The Prodigal Son." This son goes to his father and says, "Give me my inheritance."

Now, that was unthinkable. Jesus is telling a story that is shocking to the audience. He's already got their attention. With the lost sheep, they think, "Okay, I get it," and with the lost coin, "Alright, I get that." However, the lost son is not something they want to hear.

You don't go to your father while he's still alive and say, "Give me my inheritance." You only receive that after your father is dead! So, this son is practically saying, "Dad, I wish you were dead! Let's not wait any longer. Let's get this over with! Give me my portion of the inheritance that I am going to receive anyway when you die." Shockingly, in the story, the father does it; he gives the money to his son.

The son then leaves on a long journey for a far country. The implication is that he goes to a Gentile country. He leaves his Jewish family, his peers, his priest, and his people. He steps out of his religious zone, if you will.

There, in that far country, the son wastes all that money with riotous living. It's bad enough that he has asked for the money in advance. Now, he wastes it all. This is unthinkable and unconciousnable to the Jewish audience that's listening to Jesus tell this story.

Then, the Scripture goes on to say in Luke 15:14-15 that circumstances got worse, *"And when he had spent all* (his money), *there arose a mighty famine in that land; and he began to be in want. And he went and joined himself to a citizen of that country; and he sent him into his fields to feed swine."* When the famine arises, the son is financially broke. He is in ruins. He finally ends up working for a man feeding swine. Pigs are considered unclean by kosher dietary laws. The reaction would be, "A Jewish boy like you feeding the hogs—you've got to be kidding me!"

The audience is thinking, "This is terrible. What a horrible son this is!"

Worse yet, he is so hungry that he wants to eat the food they're feeding to the hogs. Jesus has deliberately made this story as shocking as he possibly can.

Yet, the greatest shock is yet to come in the story. Eventually, the boy came to his senses. Luke 15:17-19 says, *"And when he came to himself, he said, How many hired servants of my father's have bread enough and to spare, and I perish with hunger! I will arise and go to my father, and will say unto him, Father, I have sinned against heaven, and before thee, And am no more worthy to be called thy son: make me as one of thy hired servants."*

The son realizes, "I'm starving. I'm living with the pigs. I'm in this pitiful condition, yet my father's own servants eat better than I do. I know what I'll do. I'll go to my father and beg him to let me be one of his servants. I don't deserve to be one of his children any longer."

Typically, in an ancient Jewish family, if a son had behaved like this, the father would pronounce him dead. They would hold a mock funeral and would never talk about that son again as if he were alive. They would go on as though he does not exist.

For this son to even go back and beg to be a servant is to take a great risk of rejection. Yet, in Jesus' shocking story, the greatest surprise is yet to come. Verse 20 says, *"But when he was yet a great way off, his father saw him, and had compassion, and ran, and fell on his neck, and kissed him."* In an ancient family like that, the father would have never done that. Typically, a father with a rebellious son would have sat in the house waiting for the son to come and beg his forgiveness. He may or may not have given it. It's the mother who would've been out looking for the son.

In this story, the father behaves like the mother. The father is the one who was out on the road every day looking for the lost son hoping that he will come home. When the father sees his son, he runs to him with a heart of love and compassion. The father says to him, "No, you're not going to be my hired servant! You're my son!" In Verse 24, the father says, *"For this my son was dead,*

and is alive again; he was lost, and is found. And they began to be merry."

He takes him into the family with full rights and privileges. He tells the servants to put the best robe on him, a ring on his finger, and shoes on his feet. He tells them to slay the fatted calf so they can have a party and rejoice.

This is the **heart of God**. This is the heart that Jesus wants to communicate to all of those self-righteous Pharisees of His generation and of our generation. God is still in the process of saving the lost—redeeming those who have ruined their lives. He is saying to you and me, "There's still hope. There's still an opportunity. Don't live in the pig pen of life. Get up! Run to the Father!"

The Father is running to you. Don't miss His love. You can spend an entire lifetime running away from the God who loves you when, in reality, the Father is waiting for you even today to say it's time to come home to the Father's love. It's time to come home to the Father's blessings. It's time to come home and have a party. It's time to rejoice! This son of mine that was lost is found!

If you're lost, God is looking for you. God is seeking you. You need to be found. You will find yourself when you…

allow God to accept you, forgive you, embrace you, and love you!

CHAPTER 7
HIS MIRACLES

Location: Capernaum & the Region of Galilee, Circa A.D. 30/33

"And they went into Capernaum; and straightway on the sabbath day he entered into the synagogue, and taught. And they were astonished at his doctrine: for he taught them as one that had authority, and not as the scribes. And there was in their synagogue a man with an unclean spirit; and he cried out, Saying, Let us alone; what have we to do with thee, thou Jesus of Nazareth? art thou come to destroy us? I know thee who thou art, the Holy One of God. And Jesus rebuked him, saying, Hold thy peace, and come out of him. And when the unclean spirit had torn him, and cried with a loud voice, he came out of him. And they were all amazed, insomuch that they questioned among themselves, saying, What thing is this? what new doctrine is this? for with authority commandeth he even the unclean spirits, and they do obey him. And immediately his fame spread abroad throughout all the region round about Galilee."

MARK 1:21-28

The miracles of Jesus are not simply about Him displaying what He can do. We know the Son of God has power over nature, power over Satan, and power over death, but more than that, He is the Savior with a heart of compassion. He weeps when we weep. He cares about the things we care about. He loves you like no one will ever love you. He has done for you what no one has ever done for you. All of His miracles are merely to attest to the message and the Messenger—that He is indeed the Messiah, the Lord, the King, the Savior, the Lord of Life, and the Conqueror of Death.

It's sunrise on the Sea of Galilee, and around these shores and in the villages of Migdal, Capernaum, Bethsaida and Chorazin, a 30-year-old Jewish carpenter from Nazareth begins to speak of a coming kingdom. His message and His ministry will change our understanding of the divine nature of God.

Eyewitness accounts of Jesus teaching in the synagogues testify to His unusual command of the Holy Scripture. No one had

Sunrise on the shoreline of the Sea of Galilee taken from Capernaum

ever heard teaching like this; Jesus speaks with power and authority. It is becoming clear to the people of Galilee that Jesus is more than just a teacher of the Law, as Mark recalled in his Gospel in Mark 1:21-28:

> And they went into Capernaum; and straightway on the sabbath day he entered into the synagogue, and taught. And they were astonished at his doctrine: for he taught them as one that had authority, and not as the scribes. And there was in their synagogue a man with an unclean spirit; and he cried out, Saying, Let us alone; what have we to do with thee, thou Jesus of Nazareth? art thou come to destroy us? I know thee who thou art, the Holy One of God. And Jesus rebuked him, saying, Hold thy peace, and come out of him. And when the unclean spirit had torn him, and cried with a loud voice, he came out of him. And they were all amazed, insomuch that they questioned

among themselves, saying, What thing is this? what new doctrine is this? for with authority commandeth he even the unclean spirits, and they do obey him. And immediately his fame spread abroad throughout all the region round about Galilee.

It is the miraculous nature of Jesus that draws attention to His message. He performs over 30 miracles in Galilee as He moves from village to village. The miracles of Jesus bring healing and hope to the people He encounters. The miracles also amaze His closet followers, the disciples, who will later testify to Jesus as far more than a great teacher or even a prophet. They will give their lives for the One they were convinced was the Son of God.

The Feeding of the 5,000

In Mark 6:33-44, one of Jesus' greatest miracles is done on the hills of Galilee. It is here that the crowd gathers and hangs on every Word that He has to say. However, as the day wears on, the disciples say in Verses 35-36, *"This is a desert place, and now the time is far passed: Send them away, that they may go into the country round about, and into the villages, and buy themselves bread: for they have nothing to eat."* Jesus says in Verse 37, *"Give ye them to eat."* In other words, we're going to feed them ourselves.

To paraphrase the passage, the disciples say, "How? We don't have anything. There's one little boy here who brought a lunch with five loaves of bread and two little fish." The loaves would have been like pitas right out of the oven. I am sure the disciples wonder, "But what is that among so many?"

Jesus says, "Tell the men to sit down in groups of fifty," and He begins to take the bread, break it, and hand it to the disciples. They in turn take it, divide it up, and distribute it to the people. It's a miracle of multiplication as the 12 disciples distribute the bread and fish. Ultimately, everybody gets something to eat, and they were filled! When the people were done eating, Jesus tells the disciples to pick up the fragments that are left over, and there were 12 baskets full of fragments.

Jesus demonstrates His **power over nature** as He multiplies the bread and the fishes in the feeding of the five thousand. Some critical scholars have speculated that the feeding of the five thousand was not a miracle of multiplication at all—suggesting that the food was simply divided amongst the crowd. Yet, every single Gospel writer gives an account of this spectacular and miraculous event that everyone remembered.

A Galilee hillside landscape

His Healing Touch

The sixth chapter of Mark's Gospel says that, after the feeding of the five thousand, Jesus tells the disciples to get in a boat and go to Bethsaida. It is the hometown of some of the disciples. When Jesus arrives at Bethsaida, it's says in Mark 6:54-56, *"And when they were come out of the ship, straightway they knew him, And ran through that whole region round about, and began to carry about in beds those that were sick, where they heard he was. And whithersoever he entered, into villages, or cities, or country, they laid the sick in the streets, and besought him that they might touch if it were but the border of his garment: and as many as touched him were made whole."*

Here we see that the people began running everywhere across the countryside shouting that Jesus had come to the town. They brought out the sick people and laid them

"While we are studying the life of Jesus, remember this—real people, real places, and a real message that can change your life!"

Remains of the ancient gate and street of Bethsaida

in beds on the street. Pictured above are the remains of that first-century street. It took the archaeologists many years to finally find this place mentioned in the Bible. While we are studying the life of Jesus, remember this—real people, real places, real history, and a real message that can change your life!

The Bible says that they laid the sick in the street hoping they could just touch the border or the hem of Jesus' garment when He walked by in order to be healed, and <u>all</u> of them were healed. This demonstrates the miracle touch of Jesus and the miracles that occur when people touch Him. Sometimes in the stories of the miracles, Jesus would touch somebody; other times, they would touch Him. When you reach out with faith and say to the Lord Jesus, "Save me; forgive me; heal me spiritually; heal me physically," then you're calling on the One who did it then and can do it today!

The word "miracle" is described by the *Merriam-Webster Dictionary* as "an unusual or wonderful event that is believed to be caused by the power of God."

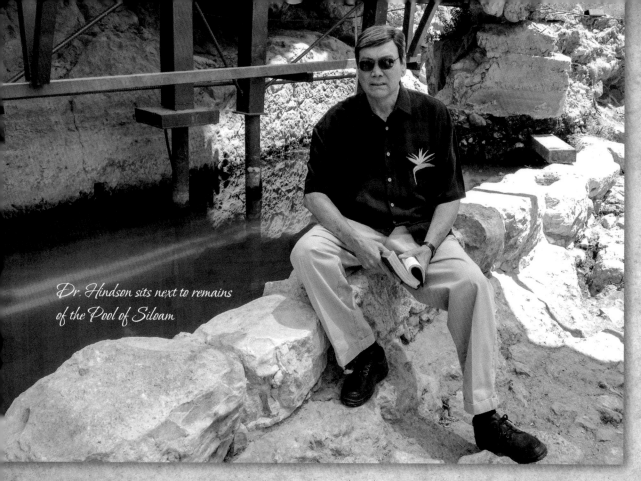

Dr. Hindson sits next to remains of the Pool of Siloam

but that the works of God should be made manifest in him. I must work the works of him that sent me, while it is day: the night cometh, when no man can work. As long as I am in the world, I am the light of the world. When he had thus spoken, he spat on the ground, and made clay of the spittle, and he anointed the eyes of the blind man with the clay."

This is a very unusual miracle that He takes the very dirt of Israel itself—in essence, of Jerusalem itself—and spreads it on the eyes of the blind man. Then, in Verse 7, Jesus says to the man, *"Go, wash in the pool of Siloam."* In the days of the New Testament, there was a large pool here with many steps. Part of it has been excavated today. It's near the water source in the Gihon Spring in Jerusalem, and it's here that the miracle took place.

The passage continues, *"He went his way therefore, and washed, and came seeing. The neighbours therefore, and they which before had seen him that he was blind, said, Is not this he that sat and begged? Some said, This is he: others said, He is like him: but he said, I am he. Therefore said they unto him, How were thine eyes opened? He answered and said, A man that is called Jesus made clay, and anointed mine eyes, and said unto me, Go to the pool of Siloam, and wash: and I went and washed, and I received sight. Then said they unto him, Where is he? He said, I know not."*

Healing the Blind & Lame

I'm sitting in the archaeological excavation of the Pool of Siloam on the edge of the city of Jerusalem. In Biblical times, this was actually part of the city itself, and it's a place where one of Jesus' most incredible miracles took place.

Jesus only performs **two miracles** in the city of Jerusalem. He heals a blind man here at the Pool of Siloam. Then, at the Pool of Bethesda, He heals a lame man. These miracles show that He is the greater Son of David—the One who can heal the lame and the blind. He is the One who can cleanse Jerusalem in order for it to be a holy city of God.

In John 9:1-6, the Bible says, *"And as Jesus passed by, he saw a man which was blind from his birth. And his disciples asked him, saying, Master, who did sin, this man, or his parents, that he was born blind? Jesus answered, Neither hath this man sinned, nor his parents:*

In John 9:13-34, the Pharisees called this man in to check on what had happened. When they discovered that the miracle had taken place on the Sabbath Day, they protested. They said, "It could not have been a miracle of God. Whoever did this to you could not be of God. He must be a sinner." In Verse 17, the once blind man said, *"He is a prophet."* Then the Pharisees called in his parents and asked them in Verse 19, *"Is this your son, who ye say was born blind? how then doth he now see?"* They said, *"We know that this is our son, and that he was born blind."* But the Pharisees wanted to know how he was healed, and the parents responded, *"By what means he now seeth, we know not; or who hath opened his eyes, we know not: he is of age; ask him."*

So in Verse 24, the Pharisees called him in again, *"Then again called they the man that was blind, and said unto him, Give God the praise: we know that this man is a sinner."* You then have that incredible response in Verse 25, *"He answered and said, Whether he be a sinner or no, I know not: one thing I know, that, whereas I was blind, now I see."*

The miracle that took place here was one of those instantaneous miracles. Blind people don't just suddenly see with clarity. Lame men don't just get up and suddenly walk away, unless it's a miracle of God that defies the very laws of nature itself.

Dr. Hindson at Pool of Siloam excavations at the city if David; the background painting depicts what the pool looked like during Jesus' time

The pool of Siloam—much of the pool is under this grove and is yet to be excavated

Then, there is this interesting tender touch in the story. Even though the leaders don't understand what has happened and are upset with the man, the man is thrilled because he has experienced the miracle. The man then goes to the temple, and the Bible says in Verse 35-38, *"Jesus heard that they had cast him out; and when he had found him, he said unto him, Dost thou believe on the Son of God? He answered and said, Who is he, Lord, that I might believe on him? And Jesus said unto him, Thou hast both seen him, and it is he that talketh with thee. And he said, Lord, I believe. And he worshipped him."*

Often you'll hear scholars say that Jesus never really claimed to be divine. Yet Jesus would dare to say, *"I and my Father are one"* (John 10:30), *"He that hath seen me hath seen the Father"* (John 14:9), *"Before Abraham was, I am"* (John 8:58). Jesus takes the sacred name of God and applies it to Himself. In John 9:35-38, He's clearly telling the once blind man that you have seen the Son of God, and it is Me.

The miracles Jesus performs in Jerusalem are very specific and are further evidence that Jesus is the Messiah, the Chosen One who would come from the line of David.

The healing of **the blind and the lame** take on special significance in light of the Old Testament account of David as he conquers the city of Jerusalem and establishes his capital.

This account is recorded in II Samuel 5:6-7, *"And the king and his men went to Jerusalem unto the Jebusites, the inhabitants of the land: which spake unto David, saying, Except thou take away the blind and the lame, thou shalt not come in hither: thinking, David cannot come in hither. Nevertheless David took the strong hold of Zion: the same is the city of David."*

When Jesus comes to Jerusalem, He seeks out the blind and the lame, and He heals them. Jesus is reminding us of the day when the city was originally conquered. It's an affirmation of the Messianic prophecies, and it's a claim to say, "I am the greater son of David." While David conquered by the sword, Jesus will conquer by compassion by healing the blind and the lame.

The blind man was healed at the Pool of **Siloam**, just below the old city of David. The lame man was healed at another popular gathering place in Jerusalem—the Pool of **Bethesda**. This was a magnificent fresh-water pool with five porches to give shade from the sun.

Ancient legends tell of the healing powers of these waters. It was said that an angel would stir the water, and if you were the first to enter the pool after the water was disturbed, you would be healed of your infirmity. It is here

Dr. Hindson in the courtyard next to the Church of St. Anne in the old city of Jerusalem near the Pool of Bethseda

that Jesus encounters the lame man, and it is here that Jesus confronts popular superstition with the real power of God.

The story was recorded in John 5:5-9, *"And a certain man was there, which had an infirmity thirty and eight years. When Jesus saw him lie, and knew that he had been now a long time in that case, he saith unto him, Wilt thou be made whole? The impotent man answered him, Sir, I have no man, when the water is troubled, to put me into the pool: but while I am coming, another steppeth down before me. Jesus saith unto him, Rise, take up thy bed, and walk. And immediately the man was made whole, and took up his bed, and walked: and on the same day was the sabbath."*

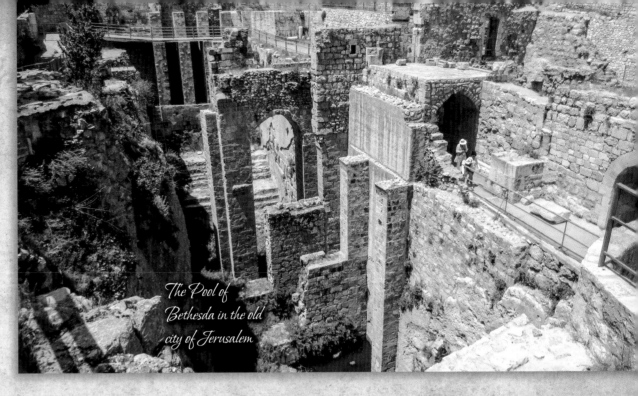

The Pool of Bethesda in the old city of Jerusalem

Jesus is dealing not only with unbelief on the part of some of the people, but all kinds of mythological beliefs, as well. In this case, Jesus is going to overcome all of that. He makes it clear to the man that you don't need somebody to put you into the pool. In Verse 8, He tells the man, *"Rise, take up thy bed, and walk."* The bed is a little mat the man is lying on. He stands up, rolls up the bed and walks away. He had been crippled for 38 years.

I once spent three months in the hospital lying dormant from a staff infection. It took me over a month to learn how to stand up again, how to get my balance, and how to even begin to take a few steps. You cannot stand up and walk immediately without an absolute miracle. In this case, a miracle of God enabled the lame man to get up and literally walk away.

When Jesus heals people, they get up and run off. In this case, the lame walks away. Yet, the Bible says it was on the Sabbath, which is a Saturday. Verses 10-11 say, *"The Jews therefore said unto him that was cured, It is the sabbath day: it is not lawful for thee to carry thy bed. He answered them, He that made me whole, the same said unto me, Take up thy bed, and walk."*

Now, imagine the attitude of the healed man. He's thrilled! This Jesus has come along and instantly and miraculously healed him. He's running home all excited to find his family when the Pharisees begin to criticize him because he's doing work on the Sabbath day. They wanted to know who did this, but the once lame man didn't know. Verses 12-13 say, *"Then asked they him, What man is that which said unto thee, Take up thy bed, and walk? And he that was healed wist not who it was: for Jesus had conveyed himself away, a multitude being in that place."* Jesus came; He healed; and He left. But that wasn't the end of the story.

Ruins of crusader church adjacent to the pool of Bethesda

The passage goes on to say in Verse 14, *"Afterward Jesus findeth him in the temple, and said unto him, Behold, thou art made whole: sin no more, lest a worse thing come unto thee."* Jesus goes out of His way to find that same man again. You see, once God does a work in our heart, He doesn't abandon us. He doesn't forget us.

Here you see the compassion of Jesus who heals a man. The Bible doesn't even tell us clearly whether the man believes anything or not. Jesus simply asks him the question, "Do you want to be healed?" Well, yes, of course. "Then take up your bed and walk." This was an instantaneous miracle that again proves that Jesus is indeed the greater Son of David who can heal the blind and heal the lame here in Jerusalem.

The Raising of Lazarus

The miracles of Jesus reach a climax with the resurrection of Lazarus. Jesus has already demonstrated His power over the demons and His power over nature. Now, He will demonstrate His power over death. Jesus will raise Lazarus from the dead. Perhaps it was to convince and encourage His disciples that His own death would not end in tragedy, but in victory—victory over death itself.

The eyewitness account is recorded in John 11. John describes Lazarus as a dear friend of Jesus. His home in Bethany, a village on the far side of the Mount of Olives, was a place of rest for Jesus and His disciples on their visits to Jerusalem.

When Lazarus becomes ill, his sisters Mary and Martha send a desperate message to Jesus to come quickly. The message is that your friend Lazarus is sick, literally sick unto death. They are making their appeal to Jesus to save His friend. However, Jesus deliberately delays His return to Bethany. His disciples are wondering why Jesus is hesitating. When they finally make their way to the village, it's been four days since Lazarus has died.

Jews believe that the spirit hovers over the body for three days after death. To the family, it appears that any hope of healing or even resurrection is lost.

Jesus arrives in the village. Martha had heard He was coming, and she rushes out to meet Him. I see Martha as the sister in charge. She's going to let Jesus know, "You're late!" Verses 21-23 say, *"Then said Martha unto Jesus, Lord, if thou hadst been here, my brother had not died. But I know, that even now, whatsoever thou wilt ask of God, God will give it thee. Jesus saith unto her, Thy brother shall rise again."*

She's thinking that Jesus is talking about the resurrection at the end of time. John 11:24-27 says, *"Martha saith unto* him, I know that he shall rise again in the resurrection at the last day. Jesus said unto her, I am the resurrection, and the life: he that believeth in me, though he were dead, yet shall he live: And whosoever liveth and believeth in me shall never die. Believest thou this? She saith unto him, Yea, Lord: I believe that thou art the Christ, the Son of God, which should come into the world."

Martha then sends for her sister Mary. Mary comes weeping and sobbing. She's crying. The mourners are still weeping and crying, too. Jesus sees the tears in the eyes of the people, and then we have that powerful verse in the Bible when you come to Verse 35. It's those two simple words, *"Jesus wept."* We see the **compassion of the Savior**. He understands what He's about to do, but He also understands the sting and pain of death, as well as what it does to us as human beings when we lose a loved one.

Jesus has asked to be taken to the tomb. As He arrives there, He shocks the people in Verse 39 and says, *"Take ye away the stone."* I am sure the people are thinking, "No, we shouldn't roll it away," but there's something irresistible about the person of Jesus. Verses 41-43 say, *"Then they took away the stone from the place where the dead was laid. And Jesus lifted up his eyes, and said, Father, I*

thank thee that thou hast heard me. And I knew that thou hearest me always: but because of the people which stand by I said it, that they may believe that thou hast sent me. And when he thus had spoken, he cried with a loud voice"—then He shouts those three simple words—*"Lazarus, come forth."*

It's been observed long ago that had Jesus simply said, "Come forth," then all the dead of all time may have come forth. However, He specifies for Lazarus to come forth. When God calls people in the Bible, He always calls them by name, personally.

God knows your name. God knows your pain. God knows what you have suffered, and God knows what you are going through. One day, God will call your name as a believer to rise again in the last day.

The Bible tells us there will come a time when Jesus will descend from the clouds of heaven, and the dead in

Christ will be raised. 1 Thessalonians 4:17 says, *"Then we which are alive and remain shall be caught up together with them in the clouds, to meet the Lord in the air: and so shall we ever be with the Lord."*

We will be with Him forever because Jesus not only has the power to give you the gift of salvation, but also of eternal life. Jesus is the Resurrection and the Life.

A replica of first-century tomb at Nazareth Village

Chapter 7 ~ His Miracles   83

Ruins of the old synagogue in Chorazin

The Condemnation of Galilee

As wonderful as the miracles of Jesus are, miracles alone don't necessarily convert the soul. These miracles attract our attention to the miracle Worker and then ultimately to His message. While many people believed in Jesus because of His miracles, there were many who still did not. He ultimately brings a message of condemnation to the cities of Galilee where He had done His greatest and most mighty works.

In Matthew 11:20-24, it explains that Jesus began to condemn the cities of Galilee where His mighty works had been done because they did not repent. Oh, they were amazed, and they wanted to be blessed by the miracle. There are a lot of people who would love for God to do a miracle on their behalf. In their mind, it's all about them; it's not really all about Him.

He brought this message in Verse 21, *"Woe."* **Woe** is the message of condemnation from the prophets of the Old Testament. It's like the ultimate "Oy Vey." Here is the message or the *Massa* in Hebrew, which means a burden, of the prophet.

Matthew 11:21-22 says, *"Woe to you Chorazin! woe to you Bethsaida! for if the mighty works had been done in you had been done in Tyre and Sidon they would have repented long ago, but I say to you it'll be more tolerable for Tyre and Sidon in the day of judgment then for you."*

In other words, God will evaluate the opportunity that people have had to hear the message of the Gospel in relation to the severity of their judgment if they reject that message. Tyre and Sidon didn't have an opportunity to really know the message like these cities had. Therefore, He said all of these cities will be judged, but it'll be much more tolerable for Tyre and Sidon than for you.

In Verse 23, He then said, *"And thou, Capernaum, which art exalted unto heaven, shalt be brought down to hell: for if the mighty works, which have been done in thee, had been done in Sodom, it would have remained until this day."* At this point, during the time of Christ, Sodom had been destroyed for nearly 2,000 years, yet Jesus says Sodom would still exist if the people had heard the kind of message and seen the kind of works that Capernaum was seeing. A time of judgment will come on these cities.

Pictured on this page are the ruins of the ancient synagogue at Chorazin, one of those three cities. All three of them—Bethsaida, Capernaum, and Chorazin—are in ruins today. Every one of those cities were cursed by the judgment of Jesus. The pronunciation of the woe against those cities has been fulfilled. Today, they are in ruins and have never been rebuilt.

The seriousness of the judgment of Christ reminds us that one day we will all stand before Him. We will either stand before Him as our Savior or as our Judge. Some will hear those terrible words, *"I never knew you: depart from me"* (Matthew 7:23).

Yet this chapter—Matthew 11—ends with an **invitation**. After all of this, Jesus still wants to reach out in love and mercy. In Matthew 11:28-30, He said, *"Come unto me, all ye that labour and are heavy laden, and I will give you rest. Take my yoke upon you, and learn of me; for I am meek and lowly in heart: and ye shall find rest unto your souls. For my yoke is easy, and my burden is light."*

Some people think, "Well, if I become a Christian, it'll be so difficult. I'll have to give up so much." No, Jesus is saying, "My yoke is easy." What He can do for you is not only forgive your sins, but also change your heart and change your life. He came that your joy might be full.

Judgment or blessing? Condemnation or rest? It's really up to us and how we respond. Will we too repent and believe, or will we look at the claims of Christ and simply walk away?

I want to urge you; don't miss what Jesus has for you! He can do for you what no one else will ever be able to do.

Nobody loves you like He loves you! Nobody cares like He cares!

Capernaum column depicting menorah an ancient symbol of Israel

The Capernaum ruins

CHAPTER 8
HIS KINGDOM & CHURCH

Location: Region of the Decapolis (Caearea Philippi), Circa A.D. 32/33

> "*When Jesus came into the coasts of Caesarea Philippi, he asked his disciples, saying, Whom do men say that I the Son of man am? And they said, Some say that thou art John the Baptist: some, Elias; and others, Jeremias, or one of the prophets. He saith unto them, But whom say ye that I am? And Simon Peter answered and said, Thou art the Christ, the Son of the living God.*"

MATTHEW 16:13-16

ome with me as we go around this region from Nazareth to Capernaum to Bethsaida to Chorazin to all of the places where Jesus came, preached, healed and touched the lives of people and ultimately changed their lives forever.

It has been nearly three years since the stranger from Nazareth first appeared on the shores of the Sea of Galilee. It was here in the fishing villages of Capernaum, Bethsaida, and Chorazin that this mysterious Rabbi recruited His closest followers. They were fishermen and tradesmen whom history remembers simply as the disciples. These men eventually come to know this Stranger from Nazareth as far more than a great teacher.

His name in their Hebrew tongue is *Yeshua*, meaning the One who saves. They will address Him as Master. They will abandon everything they have to follow Him.

Over the past three years, the disciples have made many journeys with Jesus as He has moved from town to town throughout the region of Galilee. They have been with Him as He has taught in the synagogues and as He has preached to large gatherings on the hillsides or by the sea.

They have also made the journey into Judea and made *Aliyah* or "going up" to Jerusalem, as any good Jew would do during the pilgrim feast of Israel, but by far, the most unusual journey that the disciples will ever make is the one that will take them far into the high mountains of northern Israel.

Late in His ministry, Jesus leads the disciples to one of the 10 cities established under Greek rule known collectively as the Decapolis. These are centers of Greek and Roman culture in a region that is otherwise very Semitic. The city that Jesus has chosen is Banias, and it sits at the base of Mount Hermon, Israel's tallest mountain. At the time of Jesus, Banias is also known as **Caesarea Philippi**, and it is the site of a pagan shrine.

For the disciples, this journey must have seemed ridiculous. Why would Jesus lead them to a Gentile city? And it's not just any Gentile city, but it's one that's established as a pagan shrine. But this is where

An ancient column that was part of the temple complex built for the pagan god, Pan, at Caesarea Philippi (aka Banias)

Jesus will challenge His disciples, asking them who they think He really is.

He is about to reveal to them His true identity and the sacrifice He will make when He returns to Jerusalem.

Here in this pagan capital among the Gentiles, Jesus will challenge His followers to establish an entirely new order—the church.

If you have your Bible, take it and turn to Matthew 16:13-16:

> *When Jesus came into the coasts of Caesarea Philippi, he asked his disciples, saying, Whom do men say that I the Son of man am? And they said, Some say that thou art John the Baptist: some, Elias* (Elijah)*; and others, Jeremias* (Jeremiah)*, or one of the prophets. He saith unto them, But whom say ye that I am? And Simon Peter answered and said, Thou art the Christ, the Son of the living God.*

The disciples recognized early on that Jesus is the Son of God. Peter now affirms that statement of faith on behalf of all of the apostles. Then, Jesus says to him in Matthew 16:17-18:

> *And Jesus answered and said unto him, Blessed art thou, Simon Barjona: for flesh and blood hath not revealed it unto thee, but my Father which is in heaven. And I say also unto thee, That thou art Peter, and upon this rock I will build my church; and the gates of hell shall not prevail against it.*

The word **church** in the Greek New Testament—*ekklesia*—is built on two words: *ek*, which means from, and *kaleo*, which means to call. In other words, the meaning of *ekklesia* is to call out from the world a new society—the church. The churches are a called out assembly. Jesus was saying, in essence, I'm going to build a brand new kind of synagogue, a brand new assembly—the church.

The church is announced here for the very first time. Jesus says that He will build His Assembly, and the gates of hell will not prevail against it. Many people in the ancient world actually thought a particular spot in Caesarea Philippi was literally the gates of hell. You can see it pictured on this page. In ancient times, the steam burst right out of the rock where the beginning of the Jordan River starts in the springs of the Banias. When the steam came up, they assumed it was coming up from hell itself.

The headwaters of the Jordan river at Caesarea Philippi (Banaias)— This area was the epicenter of pagan worship in the time of Christ

So Jesus interestingly brings His disciples to this very Gentile place—to the very place that people assume is the gates of hell. He announces, *"I will build my church; and the gates of hell shall not prevail* (be able to stand up) *against it"* (Matthew 16:18).

People read the text as though hell is attacking the church. I remind you that you don't attack with gates; you defend with gates. Jesus pictures hell or hades on the defensive and the church on the aggressive. He's eventually going to commission His disciples to go into all the world and preach the Gospel to all nations, and the gates of hell will not be able to prevail against it.

God will call people out of every nation on the planet unto Himself, as He builds a worldwide global church through a process of global evangelization and global engagement. In this passage, Jesus makes the statement to the disciples, *"Upon this rock I will build my church"* (Matthew 16:18).

He was undoubtedly standing right in the vicinity of "the gates of hell" in Caesarea Philippi with the giant rock face of the cliffs behind Him. Yet, it's not that rock on which Christ builds His church, and it's not on Peter as the rock. It's on the rock of that confession by Peter that Jesus is the Christ, the Son of God.

The cave believed to be the entrance to Hades (the gates of hell) at Caesarea Philippi

You can look at Jesus and say to yourself, "Well, I agree that He was a great teacher. His parables were incredible. His miracles were extraordinary—almost unexplainable. He was a great person." Some would say, "He should not have been crucified." Even the Jewish people who are not Christian believers will say, "They should never have crucified Jesus."

Beyond all of that, is He is more than a good man, more than a great teacher? Peter said yes. He's the Messiah, the Anointed One. He is the Son of God, which is *Ben Elohim* in Hebrew.

He's not just *Ben Ha adam*, which means the Son of man. He's also the Son of God. Jesus will use both terms to refer to Himself because He's fully human and yet fully divine.

Upon the rock of that testimony, Jesus will build His church, and the gates of hell will not prevail against it.

Then, He said to the disciples in Matthew 16:19, *"And I will give unto thee the keys of the kingdom of heaven: and whatsoever thou shalt bind on earth shall be bound in heaven: and whatsoever thou shalt loose on earth*

Snow-covered Mount Hermon, Israel's tallest mountain and a possible site of the transfiguration of Jesus

was consider a holy place in pagan mythology. The proximity of Banias and this mountain has led some to speculate that this may well be the site of the transfiguration of Jesus.

The pagan city of Banias or Caesarea Philippi is certainly significant to Christians. This is where Jesus will challenge His disciples as to His true idenity and purpose. It is here in these mountains that Jesus will describe the "calling out" or the assembly of what is today the church.

Jesus has brought the disciples here to make a bold statement. Banias is a place of contrasts between the mythology of man's creations and the truth that is the Word of God. In a place that erects a shrine to Pan, as the god of shepherds, Jesus appears as One who says, *"I am the good shepherd"* (John 10:11). In a place that was thought to be a gateway to the underworld, Jesus proclaims He will build His church, and that nothing will stand in its way—not even the pagan ideology that was represented so powerfully in the city of Banias.

Historians would later report that the god, Pan, was rumored to have died either shortly before or at the time Jesus makes His pilgrimage to Banias (Caesarea Philippi). Worship of Pan and the other gods of Greek and Roman mythology began to die out in practice early in the First Century.

shall be loosed in heaven." He didn't mean that they could determine who would go to heaven and who would go to hell. He means that the disciples are to go out and preach the Gospel based on that confession of faith—that I am the Christ, the Son of God. On the basis of the preaching of the Gospel, either people will be saved and, therefore, loosed from the bondage of sin, or they will remain bound in their sins. Their destiny will be determined by their response—it's either heaven or hell.

As stated earlier, Jesus has lead His disciples to the remote mountain city of Banias, which is also known as Caesarea Philippi. Here a pagan shrine is built at the entrance to a cave that has been long believed to be a portal into the underworld of Hades.

The woods surrounding the cave were thought to be the dwelling place of the god, Pan, who was half man and half goat and was said to be the god of shepherds. The mere sight of him was thought to create an uncontrollable fear or panic.

Caesarea Philippi sits at the foot of what is today called Mount Hermon. It is Israel's tallest mountain. This mountain, like Banias itself,

The city of Banias, once venerated as a pagan shrine, will become a significant Christian center in the region.

The announcement of the church was something brand new. The disciples were waiting for the coming of the Kingdom of God. Suddenly, Jesus announces that He will build His church and send His message to the whole world, and the gates of hell will not prevail against it.

The real turning point comes in Matthew 16:21: *"From that time forth began Jesus to shew unto his disciples, how that he must go unto Jerusalem, and suffer many things of the elders and chief priests and scribes, and be killed, and be raised again the third day."*

They don't want to hear that. They don't want to even let that internalize in their heart and mind. It's almost as though, when you hear something you don't want to hear, you just dismiss it.

Finally, Peter took Him aside in Matthew 16:22-23: *"Then Peter took him, and began to rebuke him, saying, Be it far from thee, Lord: this shall not be unto thee."*

Peter is saying, "Don't go to Jerusalem. Don't you realize they will want to kill you there. The winds of time will shift at that moment against us."

But Jesus let Peter know that this is what God intends for Jesus to do, *"But he turned, and said unto Peter, Get thee behind me, Satan: thou art an offence unto me: for thou savourest not the things that be of God, but those that be of men."*

That hardly sounds like Peter was the rock that Jesus was going to build the church on, as this was only a few minutes later, and now He's rebuking Peter. Then, Jesus tells Peter that he doesn't understand the things of God,

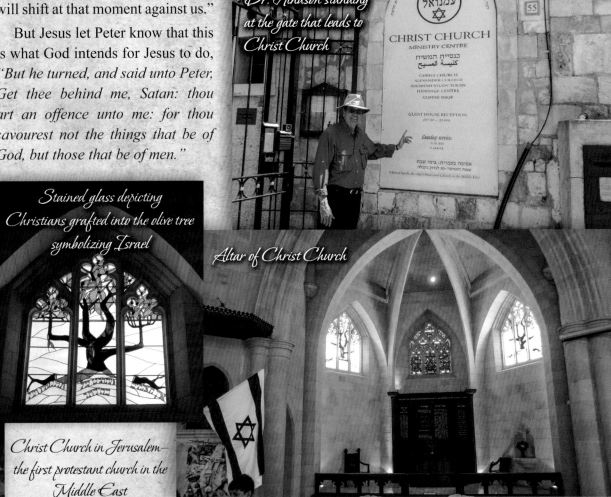

Dr. Hindson standing at the gate that leads to Christ Church

Stained glass depicting Christians grafted into the olive tree symbolizing Israel

Altar of Christ Church

Church exterior

Christ Church in Jerusalem— the first protestant church in the Middle East

but of men. On one half, Jesus tells Peter, "Blessed are you. God has revealed this truth to you." While on the other half, Jesus tells him, "Peter, you are thinking like a man. Satan is the one who talks about those kind of things in your ear. Dismiss that. That's not what I'm going to do."

Jesus said in Matthew 16:24-25: *"Then said Jesus unto his disciples, If any man will come after me, let him deny himself, and take up his cross, and follow me. For whosoever will save his life shall lose it: and whosoever will lose his life* (invest it) *for my sake shall find it."*

From that point on, Jesus makes it clear that He must come into His glory only after He is willing to suffer and die. Those were shocking words to His disciples. They were always arguing about questions like, "Who's going to be the greatest in your Kingdom? Who gets to sit next to your right hand on the throne versus your left hand on the throne? What status or position will I have?"

Over and over, Jesus has to convince them that he who is servant of all will be master of all (Mark 9:35). If you really want to be a leader in His kingdom, you must do it with humility, and you must do it with sincerity. Do it by the Grace of God.

Then He told the disciples in Matthew 16:28, *"Verily I say unto you, There be some standing here, which shall not taste of death, till they see the Son of man coming in his kingdom."* Critics of the message of the Gospel sometimes try to argue that Jesus thought He would come into the glory of His Kingdom in the lifetime of those disciples, but He did not. Therefore, He must have been wrong about what He was saying. Not at all!

> *From that point on, Jesus makes it clear that He must come into His glory only after He is willing to suffer and die*

Go to the next chapter. In Matthew 17:1, it says, *"And after six days Jesus taketh Peter, James, and John his brother, and bringeth them up into an high mountain apart."*

We're up in the **Golan Heights**. We're not far from Mount Hermon. Now, the Bible doesn't name that high mountain, but they trekked up into a high mountain, whether it was Mount Tabor or Mount Hermon. Jesus leaves the other disciples behind, presumably in Caesarea Philippi (Banias). They go up in the high mountain where Jesus is going to be transfigured before them. That Transfiguration follows the announcement of the fact that they would see Him in the Glory of His Kingdom.

When they get up the mountain, the Bible says in Matthew 17:2-8: *"And was transfigured before them: and his face did shine as the sun, and his raiment was white as the light. And, behold, there appeared unto them Moses and Elias talking with him. Then answered Peter, and said unto Jesus, Lord, it is good for us to be here: if thou wilt, let us make here three tabernacles; one for thee, and one for Moses, and one for Elias. While he yet spake, behold, a bright cloud overshadowed them: and behold a voice out of the cloud, which said, This is my beloved Son, in whom I am well pleased; hear ye him. And when the disciples heard it, they fell on their face, and were sore afraid. And Jesus came and touched them, and said, Arise, and be not afraid. And when they had lifted up their eyes, they saw no man, save Jesus only."*

He is transfigured before them. It is literally a metamorphosis. He is transformed in the way He appears. They suddenly see Him in all of His glory. He's not a normal human being. Suddenly, it's as though the robe of flesh was torn away, and they see the glory of God—just like one would see the Shekinah glory in the Holy of Holies. His face is shining like the sun. His garment was white and glistening with bright lights.

Two witnesses, Moses and Elijah, appear and speak with Him. Moses represents the Law of the Old Testament, and Elijah represents the message of the prophets. It is as though their appearance says that we are coming to represent the Law and the prophets to give our affirmation that Jesus is the final revelation of God's truth.

Then, Peter again says the wrong thing, "Lord, it's really good for us to be here. We should build three tabernacles, one for You, one for Moses, and one for Elijah." Suddenly, God the Father speaks from heaven and says, "This is my beloved Son. Listen to Him." The testimony of the disciples had been, "You're the Christ, the Son of the living God." Now, the testimony of the voice of God Himself is, "This is my Son listen to Him."

Suddenly, Moses and Elijah vanish. The bright cloud overshadows them, and the voice of God speaks to them. At this point, the disciples are so afraid that they fall on their faces on that mountaintop. Jesus has to say to them, *"Arise, and be not afraid."* They lift up their eyes.

In essence, He was saying to them that when we go to Jerusalem, I will ultimately die. The prophet Daniel said so in Daniel 9:26. The Messiah will one day be cut off, which means He will be killed. Elijah had looked forward to the time when trouble would come

in the distant future and when Israel would again be under the judgment of God as she was in the days of old.

Isaiah the prophet said of the Messiah that He will be crushed with the weight of our sins (Isaiah 53:5) and ultimately will die like a lamb going to the slaughter on our behalf (Isaiah 53:7).

What this incident is saying to you and me, as it said to the disciples back then, is that Jesus is no ordinary human being. Jesus is God incarnate. He is God in sandals, if you will. He is God in a robe—God on foot. He is God who came down from heaven, born among men so that He might speak to men. He came to die as a man, rise as God, and ascend to heaven. He has promised that one day He will return and receive us unto Himself.

We've looked at the parables of Jesus and the miracles of Jesus. He is an incredible teacher. He is a powerful individual. He has an irresistible sense of His presence. When

Dr. Hindson standing near the Joffa Gate of the old city of Jerusalem

people are in the presence of Jesus, they realized, "If I can just hear Him, my life will be changed. If I can just touch Him, I will be healed. I will be transformed." He stands before the disciples and simply says, "Follow Me," and they leave their nets.

Matthew sits at the tax collector's table in Capernaum on the great Northern Road that leads from Galilee to Damascus, and Jesus walks up to the tax table, looks at Matthew, and says, "Follow me." Matthew leaves the money and walks away with Jesus. His name had been Levi. That's the name of the family of the priest. He is supposed to be a priest. Instead, He is a backslidden Jew who has been a collaborator with the Romans. He is a publican, not just a public servant. This idea is a negative one in the minds of the Jewish people of Jesus' day. These publicans are willing to extort money from their own people for their own benefit so that they can get rich.

Jesus tells Matthew to forget the money and follow Him. Matthew gets up and follows. The disciples were unbelievable individuals from ordinary backgrounds and, in some cases, totally unspiritual backgrounds. Yet Jesus confronted them and said, "Follow Me."

I don't know what your background is or what God may be saying to you as you study the life of Christ, but the call of Jesus is always the same—"Come! Leave it all behind, and follow me."

Even if you have to take up your cross, follow Christ. Being a disciple is not an easy process. Being a disciple doesn't mean everything's going to go well in your life from that point on. Yes, God may bless you greatly, but God may also allow each of us to go through difficult times, persecution, and trouble. I'm convinced He'll keep us from the great day of tribulation that is yet to come, but that doesn't mean that we're not going to suffer difficulties in the meantime.

In all of the challenges of life, the power of the Gospel message is God loves you, and Jesus can change you. However, you have to say, "Yes, I will go and follow you."

At the time Jesus visits Banias, it has been renamed Caesarea Philippi. The name comes from both Augustus Caesar and Herod Philip, the tetriarch and son of Herod the Great. It is a Gentile city with pagan roots and has a Gentile population that will ultimately come under the influence of the Gospel, which Jesus intends to be preached to all the Gentile Nations. People in the ancient world understand that kings are destined to reign on a throne. They do not understand that this King is destined to die.

When you look at the prophecies in the Old Testament, you realize that the Messiah is going to ride into town on a donkey, and Jesus does. He is going to be betrayed for 30 pieces of silver, and He is. Ultimately, His own disciples, the sheep, are going to be scattered because the shepherd would be temporarily taken from them. When Jesus goes to the cross to die, as far as the disciples are concerned, their hopes and dreams of the Kingdom are now gone. They are crushed, but when He rises from the dead, they don't know what to think. He's alive—now what?

Yet, after the resurrection and the 10 appearances that Jesus makes to the disciples, He takes them to the Mount of Olives. As He is about to ascend into heaven, we see the disciples say in Acts 1:6: *"When they therefore were come together, they asked of him, saying, Lord, wilt thou at this time restore again the kingdom to Israel? And he said unto them, It is not for you to know the times or the seasons, which the Father hath put in his own power."*

Now, some people confuse this and think— "Well, the church is now the new Kingdom, and Israel has been replaced."

Jesus rules from heaven in the hearts of believers, but the church is not a theocracy. It's not a literal kingdom of God on earth, as was Israel in ancient times, nor will the Millennial Kingdom be in the future. Jesus could have clarified all of that by saying to the disciples, "You don't get it. The church is the new Kingdom. Go build the Kingdom." But no, that's not what He said. He said, *"It is not for you to know the times or the seasons"* (Acts 1:6)—in other words, not now, later! The literal Kingdom will come when He returns.

We don't know the time of Jesus' coming. He tells us Himself that no one knows the day or hour of His coming. We do know what we're supposed to be doing in the meantime.

We're to take the message of the **Good News** of the love of God, the grace of God, the blood shed by Jesus' death on the cross that paid for our sins, and His triumphal resurrection. That's the message that can reconcile people from every culture—the Muslim and Jew, the Christian and the atheist, the person from Asia, Africa, Europe, America, and Latin America. It doesn't matter who you are or where you're from. Jesus came to be a Savior for all, and the church opens its doors to all who will believe.

As the early Christians receive the baptism of the Holy Spirit and are empowered by the Spirit to testify and witness of Jesus Christ, thousands begin to be saved. They profess faith in Christ. They are baptized in water as a testimony of the death and resurrection of Christ. Then, they go forth with new life to serve Him and have done so for 21 centuries.

Christians from all over the world are testifying to the truth of the message of the Gospel. They are testifying to the truth of the risen Lord that Jesus Christ indeed is the Messiah. He is the Son of God. He is the Lord, and He is the King of kings. We are citizens of Christ's spiritual kingdom as He rules from heaven in our hearts and lives.

One day, we will literally reign and rule with Him on earth in His Millennial Kingdom in the future. The real question for you and me to answer is, is He going to be King of your life? Is He going to be the Lord and Master of your heart and soul? As you consider the claims of Christ, you have to answer that question. Who is He? Is He a liar who said He was God when He wasn't? Is He a lunatic who thought He was God when He wasn't? Or is He really Lord and Master?

C. S. Lewis and G. K. Chesterton both said, "You can dismiss Him as a heretic, pity Him as a lunatic…

or you can bow your knees before Him and say, 'My Lord and my God!'"

CHAPTER 9
ANSWERING HIS CRITICS

Location: Jerusalem, Circa A.D. 33

"And a very great multitude spread their garments in the way; others cut down branches from the trees, and strawed them in the way. And the multitudes that went before, and that followed, cried, saying, Hosanna to the son of David: Blessed is he that cometh in the name of the Lord; Hosanna in the highest. And when he was come into Jerusalem, all the city was moved, saying, Who is this? And the multitude said, This is Jesus the prophet of Nazareth of Galilee."

MATTHEW 21:8-11

Spring has returned to Israel, and as the days lengthen and the wild flowers bloom, thoughts soon turn to plans for *Pesach* or **Passover**.

Passover is the commemoration of the Hebrew Exodus from Egypt. Its annual observance was a mandate from the Torah. At the time of Jesus, it remains as one of the three pilgrimage feasts of Israel, and it is a time when all able bodied Jews want to travel to the great temple in the Holy City of Jerusalem.

His Arrival in Jerusalem

In A.D. 33, Jesus and His followers are among the thousands who are making their way to the Holy City. This Passover marks the climax of Jesus' life and ministry. He has spent the last three years teaching in the synagogues and public places in Galilee.

His reputation as a great speaker and miracle worker has made Him a sensation among the people of the region. It has also garnered the attention of the ruling elites in Jerusalem—to them, Jesus was a threat.

Jesus' popularity in Galilee means that He can move freely from town to town without concern for His safety. For Him to come to Jerusalem and to do so on the high and holy days of Passover is to risk a confrontation with religious leaders, especially those involved in the temple worship.

As Jesus makes His way to Jerusalem, word of His arrival spreads, and there is great anticipation of what He might say or do when He arrives. Matthew 21:1-11 says:

> And when they drew nigh unto Jerusalem, and were come to Bethphage, unto the mount of Olives, then sent Jesus two disciples, Saying unto them, Go into the village over against you, and straightway ye shall find an ass tied, and a colt with her: loose them, and bring them unto me. And if any man say ought unto you, ye shall say, The Lord hath need of them; and straightway he will send them. All this was done, that it might be fulfilled which was spoken by the prophet, saying, Tell ye the daughter of Sion (Zion), Behold, thy King cometh unto thee, meek, and sitting upon an ass, and a colt the foal of

These flowers grow atop a modern-day wall that frames the City of David Excavtion, and the wall pictured in the distance is the nearby wall of the city of Jerusalem

an ass. And the disciples went, and did as Jesus commanded them, And brought the ass, and the colt, and put on them their clothes, and they set him (Jesus) thereon. And a very great multitude spread their garments in the way (on the road); others cut down branches from the trees, and strawed them in the way. And the multitudes that went before, and that followed, cried, saying, Hosanna to the son of David: Blessed is he that cometh in the name of the Lord; Hosanna in the highest. And when he was come into Jerusalem, all the city was moved, saying, Who is this? And the multitude said, This is Jesus the prophet of Nazareth of Galilee.

A model of the temple, known as the Herodian Temple, as it was at the time of Jesus, located in the Israel Museum of Antiquity

Jesus begins His journey to Jerusalem by presenting Himself as a **King of Israel** in the line of David. If that were not enough to raise the ire of the Temple authorities, what He will do next will certainly drive them to action.

Jesus Cleanses the Temple

According to witnesses, Jesus goes to the Temple where He created quite a scene. In a rare display of anger, He overturns the tables of the moneychangers. Temple worship is a major enterprise in Jerusalem, and the moneychangers have been profiting greatly from the thousands of pilgrims who exchange their money or goods for the Temple tax. Matthew 21:12-13 says, *"And Jesus went into the temple of God, and cast out all them that sold and bought in the temple, and overthrew the tables of the moneychangers, and the seats of them that sold doves, And said unto them, It is written, My house shall be called the house of prayer; but ye have made it a den of thieves."*

After His confrontation with the money-changers, Jesus then proceeds to the Temple galleries where He begins to teach to the crowd that has gathered. He has taken charge of the Temple grounds and is performing His ministry in plain sight of the religious leaders of the day.

Confrontation by Jewish Leaders

In one of the most challenging days of Jesus' life, He is confronted by all three groups of leaders of the Jewish people in one day—the Sadducees, the Pharisees, and the Herodians. The Sadducees are basically the more liberal party of Jewish leaders. They don't believe in the resurrection of the dead, in miracles, or in angels. Then you have the Pharisees, who are intensely committed to keeping the details of the Law. Finally, there are the Herodians, who want to cooperate with the Roman government and hence with the kingdom of the Herod's.

Here in this busy city of Jerusalem with all of its noise and activity, Jesus is confronted by all three groups in one day in one of the most amazing accounts in the entire Bible.

In Matthew 22:15-17, we'll follow the story along: *"Then went the Pharisees, and took counsel how they might entangle him (Jesus) in his talk. And they sent out unto him their disciples with the Herodians"*—these religious groups normally didn't get along at all with one another, but against Jesus they're united—*"saying, Master, we know that thou art true, and teachest the way of God in truth, neither carest thou for any man: for thou regardest not the person of men. Tell us therefore, What thinkest thou? Is it lawful to give tribute unto Caesar, or not?*

The **Herodians** believe that they should pay taxes to Caesar. They feel that the best way to protect Jerusalem is to cooperate with the Roman authorities. Yet they know that this is the perfect question posing a dilemma to Jesus. If He says,

"Yes, you need to pay taxes to Caesar," the Jewish people will not be happy with that answer. If He says, "No, don't pay taxes to Caesar," they can accuse Him of being a traitor to the Roman government.

Remember the setting of Matthew 22. These leaders have gone to Jesus for the specific purpose of trying to catch Him. They're trying to trick Him into His responses.

Matthew 22:18-21 continues, *"But Jesus perceived their wickedness, and said, Why tempt ye me, ye hypocrites? Shew me the tribute money. And they brought unto him a penny. And he saith unto them, Whose is this image and superscription* (who's picture and name is on the coin)*? They say unto him, Caesar's. Then saith he unto them*—almost as if He flips the coin back to them—*Render therefore unto Caesar the things which are Caesar's; and unto God the things that are God's."*

This is exactly what the Herodians were not doing. They were not really rendering unto God the things that belong to God. They wanted to cooperate with the government simply to benefit themselves.

Next, we see the **Sadducees** in Matthew 22:23-24: *"The same day came to him the Sadducees, which say that there is no resurrection, and asked him, Saying, Master,*

The Wailing Wall in the city of Jerusalem

That's highly unlikely that that actually happened. After a while somebody would have said, "I'm out of here—forget it!" But it's an example that, I think, they came up with in their theological circles to debunk the idea of the resurrection. In other words, how could there be a literal physical resurrection of the dead if in heaven you had people who had been married to somebody else?

Their question is, in the resurrection (which they don't believe in) whose would she be? Verses 28-30 say, *"Therefore in the resurrection whose wife shall she be of the seven? for they all had her. Jesus answered and said unto them, Ye do err* (you're in error), *not knowing the scriptures, nor the power of God. For in the resurrection they neither marry, nor are given in marriage, but are as the angels of God in heaven."*

Jesus is not saying that people are angels in the resurrection, but like the angels who do not marry, neither do we marry in the eternal state. He answers the question and rebukes their lack of knowledge and understanding of the truth.

Then, Jesus says to the Sadducees in Matthew 22:31-32: *"But as touching the resurrection of the dead, have ye not read*—in other words, now that we're talking about the resurrection, let me ask you a question—*that*

Moses—in the Old Testament—*said, If a man die, having no children, his brother shall marry his wife, and raise up seed unto his brother."*

This is the concept of Levirate marriage in the Old Testament. You have an example of that in the story of Ruth and Boaz. Ruth is widowed. She's looking for a *kinsman redeemer.* These Sadducees are referring to this concept, but

they make a hypothetical example out of it— an extreme example—in Verses 25-27: *"Now there were with us seven brethren: and the first, when he had married a wife, deceased, and, having no issue* (no children), *left his wife unto his brother: Likewise the second also, and the third, unto the seventh. And last of all the woman died also."*

which was spoken unto you by God, saying, *I am the God of Abraham, and the God of Isaac, and the God of Jacob?"*

Now, that's a common Jewish affirmation of their faith and their heritage. They would all agree with that. God is the God of Abraham, the God of Isaac, and the God of Jacob. Then Jesus looks at them and says in Verse 32, *"God is not the God of the dead, but of the living."*

Jesus was basically saying that if you are affirming that He is presently the God of Abraham and Isaac and Jacob, are you not affirming that they're alive? The body may be in the grave, but the spirit is in heaven.

The promise of Christ, as well as the apostles, is that one day Jesus will return, raise the dead, and reunite the dead with their spirit, which has gone on to heaven. He then dismisses the Sadducees. The Bible says in Verse 33, *"And when the multitude heard this, they were astonished at his doctrine."* You see, this conversation is not going on in a vacuum. There's a crowd of people gathered around. They are listening to what He's saying.

At this point, the **Pharisees** are finally upset enough to say, "We better go try!" The Sadducees failed. The Herodians failed. The Pharisees try next. Matthew 22:34-36 says, *"But when the Pharisees had heard that he had put the Sadducees to silence, they were*

gathered together. Then one of them, which was a lawyer, asked him a question, tempting him, and saying, Master, which is the great commandment in the law?

They want to affirm the Law. Now, remember, Jesus said very clearly that He didn't come to break the Law or destroy the Law, but to fulfill the Law (Matthew 5:17). He wants to help us understand what Moses really wanted us to know.

In Verses 37-38, *"Jesus said unto him, Thou shalt love the Lord thy God with all thy heart, and with all thy soul, and with all thy mind. This is the first and great commandment."*

Jesus is quoting Deuteronomy 6—the great *Shema. Shema Yisrael* means "Hear, O Israel." *"Hear* (listen), *O Israel: The LORD our God is one LORD."* It's the one affirmation of faith that every Jewish person will make, even at the point of death. When they know that they are facing eternity, that's the commitment of faith from the Old Testament, and that's what Jesus says is the greatest commandment.

Matthew 22:39-40 continues, *"And the second is like unto it, Thou shalt love thy neighbour as thyself. On these two commandments—* to love God with all your heart, soul, and mind

The flag of Israel proudly flies over the Jaffa gate of the old city of Jerusalem

and to love your neighbor as yourself—*hang* (hinge) *all the law and the prophets."*

It's not just the 371 laws that some people have found throughout the Old Testament. The Law really comes down to those two things. Do you really love God with all your heart and soul and mind? Do you love others as yourself?

You see, Jesus wants you to understand that the real, true religion—if you want to use that term—of the Old Testament is the heart religion. It's not just external behaviors, routines, rituals, and external sacrifices. It's really a response of the heart. God wants to change your heart, soul, and life and make you like Himself.

There needs to be a **spiritual transformation** that takes place in your heart so you can love God with all of your heart. In turn, the evidence of that salvation is that you love your neighbor as yourself. There are a lot of people who would say, "Oh, I love God, but I can't stand my neighbor. I don't like that person." Yet Jesus reminds you that how you treat others is really an evidence of what you believe about God. The Pharisees knew what He was saying.

With each one of those groups—the Herodians, the Sadducees, and the Pharisees—there is an indictment spiritually. They understand that they are in violation. The crowd of Jewish people who are listening are amazed at Jesus' teaching. They realize this is really the truth.

In Verses 41-42, Jesus asks the Pharisees a question, *"While the Pharisees were gathered together, Jesus asked them, Saying, What think ye of Christ? whose son is he?"* Now Christ is the Greek translation of the Hebrew term *Mashiach,* which means Messiah. Whose son is the Messiah? *"They say unto him, The son of David."* They all know that's a typical Messianic term. They understand from the Old Testament that the Messiah—the King who's coming—is the greater Son of David that will arrive one day.

When the blind man shouts to Jesus, *"Son of David, have mercy on me,"* in Mark 10:47, he recognizes Jesus is the Messiah. The point in that story is that if the blind man can see that Jesus is the Messiah, why can't you see that He's the Messiah?

Then Jesus says to the Pharisees, "So do you think the Messiah is the Son of David?" Their answer is, "Yes, of course!" While the answer is right He then uses their own answer to confound them.

Dr. Hindson and his family in Jerusalem

Matthew 22:43-46 says, *"He saith unto them, How then doth David in spirit call him Lord, saying, The LORD said unto my Lord, Sit thou on my right hand, till I make thine enemies thy footstool?"* (Psalm 110:1). When the Bible says, "LORD," in all caps this means *Jehovah* or *Yahweh*. So David is saying, *"Jehovah* said to my Lord," lowercase, which is *Adonai*—the Lord *Jehovah Yahweh* said to *Adonai. If David then call him Lord, how is he his son? And **no man was able to answer him** a word, neither durst any man from that day forth ask him any more questions* (they didn't dare ask Him any more questions)*."*

You might think to yourself, "Boy, when I get to heaven one day, I've got questions I'm going to ask God. What about this? What about that?" Could I remind you that God is going to ask you and me some questions. Just ask Job.

Job wanted to talk to God, and God asked Job over a hundred questions. He couldn't answer any of them. When God gives the final exam, He'll drive you right back to the truth of Scripture and right back to the truth of life itself. This is the world that God has created and made.

The Lord *Jehovah* will say to my Lord *Adonai,* "Sit at my right hand." What we find later in the New Testament is that Jesus Christ sits at the right hand of the Father on the throne, and He is co-equal with the Father.

The Bible shouts to you about the **deity of Christ**. Don't fall for people who try to say that Jesus never claimed to be God. Jesus shouts to you that He is God. *"I and the Father are one,"* (John 10:30), *"He that hath seen me hath seen the Father"* (John 14:9), and *"Know that the Son of man hath power on earth to forgive sins"* (Mark 2:10). Only God can do that. Right! That's exactly what Jesus is claiming in Mark 2:5 when He says, *"Son, thy sins be forgiven thee."* And in Verses 9-11, *"Whether is it easier to say to the sick of the palsy, Thy sins be forgiven thee; or to say, Arise, and take up thy bed, and walk? But that ye may know that the Son of man hath power on earth to forgive sins, (he saith to the sick of the palsy,) I say unto thee, Arise, and take up thy bed, and go thy way."*

The miracle is that affirmation of the miraculous nature of Christ Himself. It's not just that Jesus can do the miraculous. Jesus is the miraculous. He is God incarnate in human flesh. He's fully God and fully man. He walks among men, but He lives above men because He's God in a robe, God in sandals, God on foot. Jesus is the God who comes down into the fallen place to say to us, "I've come down to meet your need. I come to suffer and die so that ultimately I might reign and rule."

From the very beginning, Jesus understands that, even when the disciples do not and even when they have said to Him, "Don't go to Jerusalem. Everything could go wrong there."

To paraphrase Jesus' response in Mark 8, Jesus basically says, "Get behind me Satan. It was for this reason I was born and for this reason I came into the world. I must go and suffer first before I reign and rule.

Today, we know that Jesus has already suffered on the cross. He has already died. We look back with the eye of faith to what He has already accomplished. We understand that, if we put our faith and trust in Him, that is the basis of real salvation. That's what brings blessing and glory not only to the Lord Himself, but also into our hearts.

The Story of Nicodemus

Not all of the leaders reject what Jesus has to say. In fact, one of the most gripping and moving stories in all of the New Testament is found in the third chapter of the Gospel of John. It is the story of a man named Nicodemus, a ruler of the Jewish people and Pharisee, who came to Jesus by night to talk to Him.

In the cover of darkness in Jerusalem, Nicodemus, a very important person, seeks an audience with Jesus and an opportunity to talk with Him personally.

We read in John 3:1-2: *"There was a man of the Pharisees, named Nicodemus, a ruler of the Jews: The same came to Jesus by night, and said unto him, Rabbi, we know that thou art a teacher come from God: for no man can do these miracles that thou doest, except God be with him."* It's almost as though the ruler comes to give his affirmation and approval to Jesus.

Then, in Verses 3-5: *"Jesus answered and said unto him, Verily, verily, I say unto thee, Except a man be born again, he cannot see the kingdom of God."* Like most of us Nicodemus' response was, *"How can a man be born when he is old? can he enter the second time into his mother's womb, and be*

> Jesus has come to introduce people to a spiritual kingdom and a personal relationship with God

born?" But Jesus isn't talking about a physical birth. *"Jesus answered, Verily, verily, I say unto thee, Except a man be born of water* (physically) *and of the Spirit, he cannot enter into the kingdom of God."*

Jesus has come to introduce people to a spiritual kingdom and to a personal relationship with God Himself. This only happens through the experience of being born again by the power of the Holy Spirit.

As they discuss that issue through the night, Jesus emphasizes the importance of this spiritual renewal. The idea comes right out of the Old Testament. The prophet Ezekiel made it clear that one day God would bring His people back to the land physically, but that they would have to be then be born of the Spirit (Ezekiel 11:19). So the idea of being born again is not just a New Testament idea. It really comes from the Old Testament Scriptures, as well.

Jesus wants Nicodemus to understand that Jesus will be the agent through which that will be accomplished.

Look at John 3:7-16. Verse 7 says *"Marvel not* (don't be surprised) *that I said unto thee, Ye must be **born again**."* It's a necessity, it's not just a casual action. It's a necessity, if one is to have a personal relationship with God.

Then He explained to Nicodemus in Verse 8, *"The wind bloweth where it listeth, and thou hearest the sound thereof, but canst not tell whence it cometh, and whither it goeth: so is every one that is born of the Spirit."* When the Spirit of God moves, you see the evidence of His moving in the heart and life of a believer. When a person is born again by the power of God, he establishes a relationship with God. The fruit or basis of his salvation is the evidence of it. In other words, the root of my faith in the Word of God is evidenced by the fruit of my life. People want to see the reality

The old city of Jerusalem at night

of God alive inside of us and see the reality of Christ in us.

It is in this text in **John 3:16** that the Scripture says, *"For God so loved the world, that he gave his only begotten Son, that whosoever believeth in him should not perish, but have everlasting life."* That familiar verse is followed by Verse 17, in which the Scripture says: *"For God sent not his Son into the world to condemn the world; but that the world through him might be saved."*

Jesus didn't come to just tell us that we're sinners and that we're lost. If we are honest, we ought to know that in and of ourselves. Jesus came to give us hope, redemption, salvation, forgiveness, and transformation. He wants to change your life.

As we are studying the life of Christ, we can certainly respect all the things that He stood for. We can be captivated by the greatness of His teaching. However, ultimately, we have to be drawn irresistibly to His person—to a personal relationship with the God of heaven through the Lord Jesus Christ, who is indeed the promised Messiah. Jesus is…

the Savior of the world, the Lord, and the King, who wants to rule as King in your heart and in your life!

CHAPTER 10
JESUS PREDICTS THE FUTURE

Location: The Mount of Olives in Jerusalem, Circa A.D. 33

> "*O Jerusalem, Jerusalem, thou that killest the prophets, and stonest them which are sent unto thee, how often would I have gathered thy children together, even as a hen gathereth her chickens under her wings, and ye would not!*"
>
> MATTHEW 23:37

The real significance of the Olivet Discourse is that you and I are to be ready to meet the Lord. We can speculate all day long about when and how Jesus may return, but the promise of Jesus is, "I will come back one day. Are you watching for Me? Are you ready to meet Me when I come? Are you serving Me in the meantime?"

Maybe as you have been studying the life of Christ, you have listened to the claims of Christ and are asking yourself—is Jesus really who He says He is? Can He do what He says He could do? Can Jesus forgive my sin, save my soul, and change my life? The answer of the Bible is absolutely yes!

Jerusalem, David's capital, is the center of Jewish life and faith in Judea. This is the Holy City where the Great Temple stands. Just days before His arrest, Jesus gathers the disciples on the Mount of Olives. As they overlook the city of Jerusalem, Jesus makes a startling prediction. The Temple, the magnificent structure that was a wonder of the ancient world and is considered the most sacred place in Judaism, will be destroyed.

Dr. Hindson standing on the Mount of Olives overlooking the city of Jerusalem

Jesus reveals to the disciples a glimpse of the future—and not just their future, but also the future for all mankind. In what would later be called the Olivet Discourse, Jesus provides three warnings and gives three signs of the end of the age. Jesus also speaks of the day of His return to the city of Jerusalem as King and Ruler of the world.

Destruction of the Temple Predicted

In the picture above, I'm standing on the Mount of Olives. This is the very place where Jesus brought the disciples in those last days before Jesus would go to the cross. As Jesus walks away from the Temple and looks at the city of Jerusalem, He says in Matthew 23:37:

O Jerusalem, Jerusalem, thou that killest the prophets, and stonest them which are sent unto thee, how often would I have gathered thy children together, even as a hen gathereth her chickens under her wings, and ye would not!

Jesus comes to Jerusalem knowing that eventually it will send Him to the cross, yet He comes with love, compassion, and concern. He comes here to cast the moneychangers out of the Temple and to remind the people

of Israel that the Temple is His Father's house of prayer. It is a place Jews come to speak to God personally and to express their spiritual relationship with God, yet they have turned it into a marketplace of commercialism and personal prosperity. There was everything there but the presence of God.

As Jesus Christ—the Son of God, God Incarnate, God in person, God in sandals, God on foot—walks in this city of Jerusalem, He comes to offer Himself as the **promised Messiah**. Yet, it's here that He would be rejected. That's why He says, *"O Jerusalem, Jerusalem... how often would I have gathered they children together, even as a hen gathered her chickens under her wings* (loved you and accepted you), *but ye would not!"*

Then He says in Matthew 23:39: *"For I say unto you, Ye shall not see me henceforth, till ye shall say, Blessed is he that cometh in the name of the Lord."* That's a Messianic statement from the Old Testament.

When you say blessed is the One who comes in the Name of the Lord, and when you understand that I really am the Messiah, the Promised One who fulfills the prophecies, then you will know that I have come to be your Savior. Even now, 2,000 years later, Jerusalem is still waiting for that time when she will say, *"Blessed is he that cometh in the name of the Lord."*

As the disciples go back into the Temple, they are enamored with the building. (That ancient Temple sat right where the Dome of the Rock sits today.) As the disciples look at the magnificent structure, they're talking about the building, but Matthew 24:1-2 says: *"And Jesus went out, and departed from the temple: and his disciples came to him for to shew him the buildings of the temple. And Jesus said unto them, See ye not all these things? verily I say unto you, There shall not be left here one stone upon another, that shall not be thrown down."*

The disciples were stunned, shocked— "What?! The Temple destroyed! Every Jewish man would give his life to defend the Temple and this city. Are you predicting the judgment of God on the city of Jerusalem?"

And He was. The judgment of God is on the Temple itself. God is not the curator of a museum. God does not keep old buildings. God wants the disciples to understand—I'm concerned about your lives, your heart, and your relationship to God. The prediction would ultimately be fulfilled dramatically!

The Olivet Discourse

The Mount of Olives, also known as Mount Olivet, is a mountain ridge east of the old city of Jerusalem. It gets its name from the olive groves that once stood there. The mount has been used as a Jewish cemetery for over 3,000 years. It is believed that this is where the dead will be resurrected and judged by the God of Israel at the end of time.

The Mount of Olives is a significant place in the life and ministry of Jesus. This is where Gospel writers say that Jesus weeps over the city of Jerusalem. This is also where Jesus comes to pray before His arrest and trial before the Temple authorities.

The Mount of Olives is also where Jesus would gather His closest followers to tell them incredible things about the future. He speaks of the day when the unthinkable happens, a day when the Holy City of Jerusalem would be destroyed. The Temple, the very symbol of Jewish life and faith in Judea would be torn down and trampled over by the Gentiles.

As stated before, the disciples are absolutely shocked by everything Jesus is telling them. The Temple is going to be destroyed! They leave in stunned silence and come across the Kidron Valley to the slopes of the Mount of Olives. It is from here they are sitting and looking back on the Temple.

They come to Jesus in Matthew 24:3, and they asked him three questions: *"And as he sat upon the mount of Olives, the disciples came unto him privately, saying, Tell us, when shall these things be? and what shall be the sign of thy coming, and of the end of the world?"*

In other words, they are saying, "Lord, there are **three questions** on our minds that we want to know the answers to. *First*, when will the Temple be destroyed? *Second*, what is the sign of Your coming? Already they sense that Jesus is going to leave and return. *Third*, when are we going to finally come to the end of the age where You are going to come in power and glory to reign and rule as King?"

The temple mount of the city of Jerusalem as seen from the Mount of Olives

All that follows in Matthew 24 and 25 is our Lord's answer to those three questions. As Jesus responds to those questions, He does so in a very typical first-century, rabbinic teaching style. He mixes three warnings in with the three answers. He gives them three words of application. Then, in Chapter 25, He shares three illustrations to drive home the point.

First of all, Jesus began with one of the **warnings**. In Matthew 24:4-5, He said: *"And Jesus answered and said unto them, Take heed that no man deceive you. For many shall come in my name, saying, I am Christ; and shall deceive many."* Warning number one is **beware of false prophets**. Many will come along saying, "I'm the Christ. I'm the Messiah. I'm the Savior. I have the answer."

Indeed, in the 21 centuries of church history that have followed, there are many false prophets who have come along and tried to claim that they have a new revelation from God or a new message from God. Some have claimed to be the savior or divine one. Cult after cult after cult have made claims. Yet, I will remind you that there has probably never been a greater false prophet than Muhammad, who dared to say, "While Jesus is a prophet, I am <u>the</u> prophet! While the Bible is a word from god, the Koran is <u>the</u> ultimate word from god." The deception of his influence has left literally hundreds of millions of people trapped behind the Islamic curtain. Jesus warns us to beware of false prophets who will deceive many.

This is a scale replica of the Temple built by Herod the Great—the temple at the time of Jesus. The Herodian Temple was destroyed by the Romans in 70 A.D. This replica stands adjacent to the Israeli museum.

Then, the second warning—**wars and rumors of wars**—is found in Matthew 24:6-7, *"And ye shall hear of wars and rumours of wars: see that ye be not troubled: for all these things must come to pass, but the end is not yet. For nation shall rise against nation, and kingdom against kingdom: and there shall be famines, and pestilences, and earthquakes, in divers places."*

Note, in Verse 6, Jesus says, *"The end is not yet."* Remember the disciples had asked Him, *"And of the end of the world?"* Jesus is saying that just because there are wars, conflicts, and problems that doesn't mean the end is here. There have always been wars in a fallen world. You and I live in a fallen planet of depraved hearts where there will always be conflict and turmoil. Just because there's a crisis on one part of the planet, whether in Europe, in the Middle East, in the Far East, or in Africa, that doesn't mean it's the end of the world.

No, the end comes when the final conflicts of the end times come. That's at the very time of the end. So we shouldn't be surprised with the war on terrorism or with the crisis that we see today in the Middle East. There are many things going on that are the result of false prophets, wars, and rumors of wars. Jesus says in Matthew 24:8, *"All these are the beginning of sorrows."* So when these things begin to happen, that's just the beginning of sorrows.

The third warning that Jesus gives is all the way down in Matthew 24:36—**no one knows the time of My coming**. Jesus said, *"But of that day and hour knoweth no man, no, not the angels of heaven, but my Father only."*

> ## "Nobody knows the exact time of Jesus' coming, not even the angels"

In other words, nobody knows the exact time of My coming. Just because there's a crisis, that doesn't mean this is the end. In other words, don't fall for those false prophets today who will try to tell you, "Oh! I know the date of the Second Coming!" No, you don't!

Nobody knows the time;
So don't waste your time,
Trying to guess the time.
You need to be ready all the time,
Because Jesus could come at any time!

The three warnings were meant to caution the disciples not to run ahead of God or to panic at the circumstances, but to realize that God is on the throne. God is in control. God knows exactly what He's doing.

Then Jesus also answered the three questions—**When will the Temple be destroyed? What will be the sign of Your coming and of the end of the world?**

Jesus answered the first question in Matthew 24:15: *"When ye therefore shall see the abomination of desolation, spoken of by Daniel the prophet, stand in the holy place, (whoso readeth, let him understand:)"*

Answer number one is **the abomination of desolation**. When you see the abomination of the desolation spoken of by Daniel the prophet in Daniel 9:27 sit in the Holy place, Matthew 24:16-17 says, *"Then let them which be in Judaea flee into the mountains: Let him which is on the housetop not come down to take any thing out of his house: Neither let him which is in the field return back to take his clothes."*

In other words, what Jesus was saying to His disciples in answer to the question of when these things will happen was, "When the Gentiles dare to desecrate the Temple, run for your lives. They'll destroy the Temple."

Within 40 years, that prediction came true. The Romans eventually march into Jerusalem, take down a Jewish rebellion, and literally destroy the entire city. They tear the Temple down stone by stone, block by block, and in fulfillment of Jesus' prophesy, it becomes a stark reality.

God is trying to say to the people of Israel that it's not about the building—it's about

Me and your relationship with Me. It's all about a heart relationship. It's not about just preserving the building itself. The building will be destroyed because the power of God in salvation will come through the person of Jesus Christ. This happens when He comes to live in the heart and life of a believer. You and I become the Temple of God when God comes to dwell within us.

And then, He answered question number two in Matthew 24:21. Now, He looks down to the distant future to **a time of great tribulation**:

"For then shall be great tribulation, such as was not since the beginning of the world to this time, no, nor ever shall be."

This will be a time of trouble worse than anything the world has ever known in the past, and worse than anything the world will ever know in the future. This is the time of Great Tribulation that the Bible speaks of in both the Old and New Testament.

The Old Testament writers called it the time of *Jacob's trouble*. The Tribulation is not a time of trouble for the Church. You don't

beat up the Bride of Christ during the time of Tribulation and then take her home to the marriage in heaven. It's a time of tribulation and trouble for the people of Israel who are re-gathered back to the Promised Land. They will be anticipating the coming of "a" Messiah, but they suddenly begin to realize "the" Messiah that they have been looking for is the One who already came the first time. It's *Yeshua HaMashiach*—Jesus the Christ. He's the promised Messiah.

Now the promise is that Jesus will come the second time to save Israel and to deliver the city and the nation from the judgment that is coming in the last days in the time of great tribulation.

Then Jesus answered the third question first of all in Matthew 23:14: *"And this gospel of the kingdom shall be preached in all the world for a witness unto all nations; and then shall the end come."*

So answer number three is the **Gospel will be preached to all nations**.

Let's review the questions again. When will these things be? It will be when the Gentiles desecrate the temple. They'll destroy it, and every stone will be thrown to the ground. That was literally fulfilled in the past.

Secondly, when will we know that You have come to reign and rule? This is when the time of tribulation has come. When that tribulation comes to an end, the Scripture says in Matthew 24:29-30: *"Immediately after the tribulation of those days shall the sun be darkened, and the moon shall not give her light, and the stars shall fall from heaven, and the powers of the heavens shall be shaken: And then shall appear the sign of the Son of man in heaven: and then shall all the tribes of the earth mourn, and they shall see the Son of man coming in the clouds of heaven with power and great glory."*

At the end of the time of Tribulation, Jesus will return, split the Mount of Olives in half, and then march into Jerusalem through the Golden Gate. Then, He will reign and rule on David's throne. That promise of fulfillment is yet to come in the future. Jesus is saying to the disciples, "I will return in power and glory, but that's not going to happen this time."

Later, when Jesus ascends to heaven from the Mount of Olives, the disciples would ask Him in Acts 1:6, *"Lord, wilt thou at this time restore again the kingdom to Israel?"* Jesus responded in Verse 7, *"It is not for you to know the times or the seasons, which the Father hath put in his own power."*

In other words, Jesus is saying that they'll get the Kingdom eventually. He isn't saying that the Church is the Kingdom, because the Church is not the Kingdom. The Church is totally separate from the Kingdom. The Kingdom will only come when the King comes back to reign and rule. At that time, Jesus will come and split the Mount of Olives in half.

In the meantime, the Gospel of the Kingdom is to be preached in all the world. Today, we are a part of the **spiritual kingdom**, where Jesus reigns and rules from heaven in the heart and life of every believer, so that you and I are citizens of that heavenly Kingdom.

It's not an earthly Kingdom. That's why He'll tell Peter in the Garden of Gethsemane to put up his sword (Matthew 26:52-54). No one is going to bring His Kingdom to reality through force and power, but through moral, spiritual and intellectual persuasion. That's how you bring in the Kingdom of God.

Jesus has answered the three questions and has given the three warnings. He now ends the chapter with three words of **application**. At the end chapter in Matthew 24:42, He said, *"Watch therefore: for ye know not what hour your Lord doth come."* In other words, keep an eye on the sky. **Keep watching for Me to come.** Keep looking for Me to come.

Then the second word of application in Matthew 24:44: *"Therefore be ye also ready: for in such an hour as ye think not the Son of man cometh."* **Be ready for Me to come.** Each of us is to live a life of constant readiness where your heart and life is right with God,

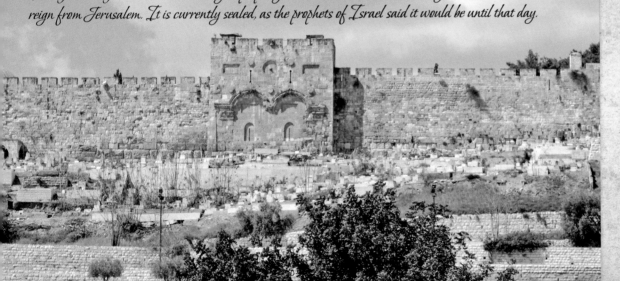

The Golden Gate is where, according to prophecy, the Messiah will enter the city when He arrives to reign from Jerusalem. It is currently sealed, as the prophets of Israel said it would be until that day.

and where you are ready to go at any moment should the Savior come and call you home.

Be ready whether it is when He returns in the Rapture to raise the dead and catch up the living, or if you and I step from this life to the next in death. We have to know that I'm ready to go. I'm ready to meet the Savior.

All of us are going to face Him one day, either as our Savior or as our Judge.

Then, the third word of application is in Matthew 24:46: *"Blessed is that servant, whom his lord when he cometh shall find so doing."* In other words, **keep serving Me until I come**.

These are three words of simple application that really apply to all of us—Be watching for Jesus to come; be ready for Him to come; and in the meantime, keep serving until He comes. Whatever it is God has called you to do, gifted you to do, and equipped you to do, do it to the glory of God, and keep on doing it until Jesus comes.

If you're a teacher, keep teaching until Jesus comes. If you're a preacher, keep preaching, "Thus saith the Lord," until Jesus comes. If you're a servant, keep serving until Jesus comes. If you're an usher, keep ushering until Jesus comes. If you are an elder, keep being an elder and grow older until Jesus comes. Keep serving until He comes.

If you're a singer, keep singing. If you are working with young people, keep doing so. In other words, whatever it is the Lord wants you to do to build His church in the years ahead, keep serving faithfully until He comes to call us home. Watch for Jesus to come. Be ready for Him to come. Keep serving until He comes.

In the photo, I'm sitting right in the midst of the fulfillment of Jesus' prophecy that every stone of the Temple would be cast down. These are those Temple stones. In 70 A.D., when the Roman army destroyed the second temple, they literally threw these stones down from the Temple mount. They landed here on the first-century street. The street is buckled with the impact of the weight of those stones.

You can literally come to Jerusalem today and touch the fulfillment of Jesus' prophecy—those stones. They are a reminder of the fact that there once was a beautiful Temple here on the Temple Mount. It's the same Temple that amazed Jesus' disciples. Yet, Jesus shocked and stunned those disciples when He said that every stone of this Temple would be cast down. In the disciples' minds, that seemed like an impossibility—an outrageous claim.

Yet, Jesus understood clearly that God is not the curator of a museum. He doesn't

Dr. Hindson sitting among the stone ruins that were cast down from the temple mount just as Jesus predicated

keep old buildings. When the building no longer represents Him and His purpose in our lives and hearts, the building can be removed because God is concerned about living in the heart and life of His people. That's why the Christian is referred to as the temple of the Spirit of God (1 Corinthians 3:16).

When you are born again by the power of the Holy Spirit, the Spirit of God comes to live within your heart and life. This causes our spirit to come to life, so that your spirit is then co-eternal with the life of God. You and I will live forever because the God who is forever lives within us. What an amazing prediction!

Today, Christians, Jewish rabbis, and archaeologists alike agree that this is the fulfillment of what Jesus said would happen—because of Jerusalem's rejection of Him, there would come a judgment on the building. For the Jews, it was the symbol of their faith. In reality, even the Old Testament had proclaimed for us to love the Lord your God with all our heart and soul and mind. It's not about the stones. It's not even about the place.

It's all about our relationship with Him, the eternal, everlasting God who wants to give us a gift of everlasting life!

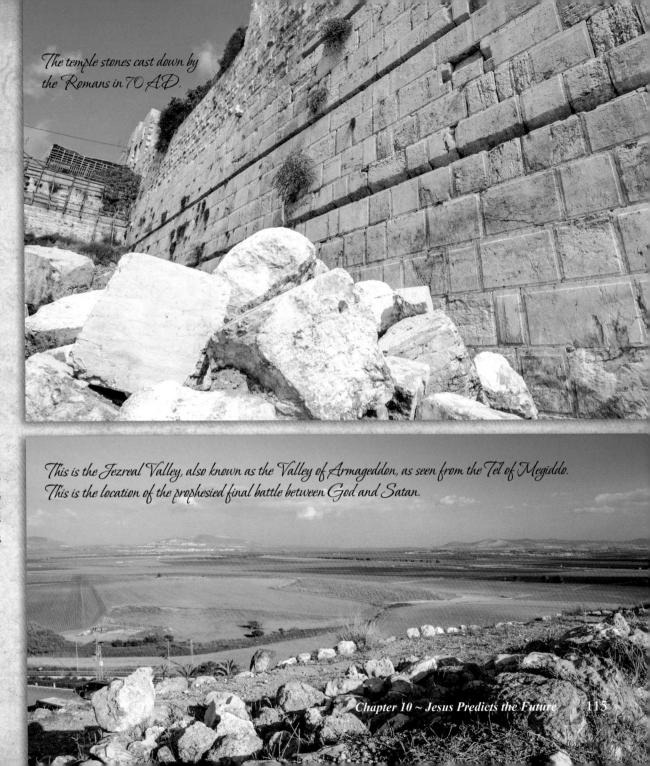

The temple stones cast down by the Romans in 70 A.D.

This is the Jezreal Valley, also known as the Valley of Armageddon, as seen from the Tel of Megiddo. This is the location of the prophesied final battle between God and Satan.

CHAPTER 11
HIS ARREST & TRIAL

Location: Jerusalem, Circa A.D. 33

" *Then cometh Jesus with them unto a place called Gethsemane, and saith unto the disciples, Sit ye here, while I go and pray yonder. And he took with him Peter and the two sons of Zebedee, and began to be sorrowful and very heavy. Then saith he unto them, My soul is exceeding sorrowful, even unto death: tarry ye here, and watch with me. And he went a little further, and fell on his face, and prayed, saying, O my Father, if it be possible, let this cup pass from me: nevertheless not as I will, but as thou wilt.* "

MATTHEW 26:36-39

n A.D. 33, Jesus will make His final pilgrimage to Jerusalem. He and the disciples will make this journey at **Passover**. Passover is the commemoration of the Hebrew Exodus from Egypt, and it's one of three great pilgrim feasts of Israel.

The events of this Passover will be the climax of Jesus' life and ministry. In seven days that will change the course of history, Jesus will be arrested, abandoned, beaten, crucified, and buried.

Yet, this week that has been called "The Passion" or "The suffering of the Christ" will not see the end of Jesus or His movement. In the greatest miracle man has ever witnessed, Jesus will emerge from His tomb alive!

At a time when Jews come to Jerusalem to remember their deliverance from "The Angel of Death" at Passover, Jesus will come to Jerusalem to turn back death itself.

His Betrayal and Arrest

In an upper room in Jerusalem, Jesus gathers His disciples for an early Passover meal. They observe the *Seder*, a ritualized meal that is a commemoration of the Hebrew Exodus from Egypt. In what will forever be remembered as the Last Supper with His disciples, Jesus presents Himself as the sacrificial Lamb of Pass-

The Garden of Gethsemane—
It was here that Jesus prayed with His
disciples and then was betrayed and arrested

over. It will be His blood that will save His followers from judgment and His body that will be broken in atonement for their sin.

After the meal, Jesus and the disciples make their way to the Mount of Olives where they will stop and pray in the Garden of the Olive Press, known as **Gethsemane**. Jesus waits for the inevitable confrontation that He knows is coming.

It is here in the Garden of Gethsemane that Jesus brings the disciples that night to get

This church is built over the ruins of what is believed to be the House of Caiaphas, the high priest, where Jesus was taken after his arrest

These steps lead up from the Kidron Valley and are remnants of the actual path Jesus would have taken the night He was arrested

the Garden of Gethsemane. That's where He and the disciples will spend the night."

While Judas is making the arrangements for the betrayal, Jesus is trying to warn the disciples of what is coming. He takes Peter, James, and John further into the inner recess of the garden and says to all the disciples on the perimeter, *"Sit ye here, while I go and pray yonder."* For those three on the inner circle, He says, *"Tarry ye here, and watch with me."* Then, the Bible tells us in Matthew 26:39, *"And he* (Jesus) *went a little further, and fell on his face, and prayed, saying, O my Father, if it be possible, let this cup pass from me: nevertheless not as I will, but as thou wilt."*

You have this location of the garden among the **olive trees**, and I wonder if those olive trees could speak what story they would tell us about those people—the temple guards and Judas—who came so close to Jesus that night

away, and yet He realizes that, before the night is over, He'll be betrayed. Judas is already at the temple making his final arrangements saying to the leaders, "I know where He will be. He will go to that garden like He always does. They'll spend the night there on the opposite side of the Valley of the Kidron there on the slopes of the Mount of Olives at

and who were face to face with the Son of God, and yet they missed Him. What a tragedy! If olive trees could weep, they would have wept that night for all that the guards, Judas, and the disciples missed. The disciples forsook Jesus and fled before the night was over.

Let's talk more about what happened that night in the garden. As stated before, Jesus takes His disciples to the Garden of Gethsemane to pray. While His disciples, who are full from their Passover meal, slumber, Jesus prays in anguish, aware that His time of pain and suffering is at hand. The temple guard is on the march, and they are coming for Jesus. They will be led to this garden by a member of Jesus' inner circle of followers. It is Judas who identifies the Rabbi from Nazareth and betrays His master with a kiss.

As the temple guards move to arrest Jesus, the loyal disciples resist. In the commotion, Peter draws a sword to fight, but Jesus tells Peter to put away his sword. Then Jesus surrenders to the temple guard. As Jesus is led away down the Kidron Valley, He passes by the ancient cemeteries at the foot of the Mount of Olives. He is on His way to the House of Caiaphas, the high priest. Peter and John follow, but at a distance, trying not to be seen by Jesus' captors (Matthew 26:47-58; John 18:15).

From the Garden of Gethsemane, Jesus was brought to the **House of Caiaphas** by the temple guards. It is in Caiaphas' courtyard that Peter ultimately faces his greatest challenge. At this point, Peter is likely feeling somewhat hurt by Jesus' statement to him in Matthew 26:52-54, *"Put up again thy sword into his place: for all they that take the sword shall perish with the sword. Thinkest thou that I cannot now pray to my Father, and he shall presently give me more than twelve legions of angels? But how then shall the scriptures be fulfilled, that thus it must be?"*

Most of the disciples had fled into the night. Jesus is left alone with His captors. He is brought to the House of Caiaphas to stand before a representative of the Sanhedrin. Not all are in attendance. In fact, Nicodemus will later protest, "Why wasn't I called?"

Now, in the middle of the night, with a trumped up charge, this group accuses Jesus of claiming that He's going to destroy the temple and say that He's preaching false truth. Finally, in Matthew 26:63, the high priest looks at Jesus and says, *"I adjure thee by the living God, that thou tell us whether thou be the Christ, the Son of God."* In other words, I put you under oath to God Himself. Are you the Messiah, the Son of God? In Mark's Gospel, it's expressed *"the Son of the Blessed,"* the Jewish way of referring to God (Mark 14:61).

And Jesus answers an emphatic yes in Mark 14:62, *" I am: and ye shall see the Son*

Statue at the House of Caiaphas depicting Christ's arrest

of man sitting on the right hand of power, and coming in the clouds of heaven." At that, the high priest rips his robes, spits at Jesus, and slaps His face. All His accusers denounce Jesus as a blasphemer.

Peter Denies Him

Out in the courtyard, Peter and John, two of the disciples are watching the proceeding going on. Peter's heart is pounding as he likely wonders, "What if they figure out that we are disciples? What if they call us up there on the balcony? What if they start to accuse us?" Suddenly, the Bible says that John, who

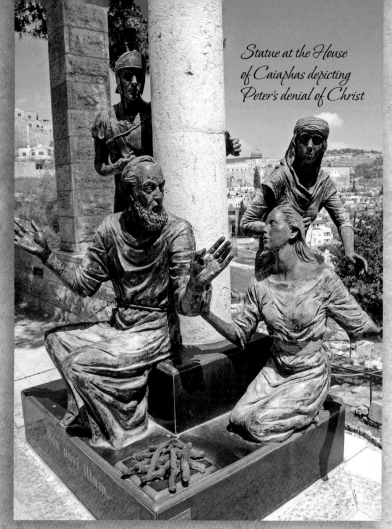

Statue at the House of Caiaphas depicting Peter's denial of Christ

knew the gatekeeper, got them entrance a little further in (John 18:15-16).

Then, in John 18:17, the girl at the gate turned to Peter and said, *"Art not thou also one of this man's disciples?"* And Peter said, *"I am not."* In Matthew 26:70, Peter says, *"I know not what thou sayest."* In other words, I don't know what you are talking about.

The first denial was to simply just play dumb. When someone asks, if you are a Christian or a believer, the response is, "Oh, I don't know. What do you mean?" You just **play dumb**, and it's a denial.

Pretty soon in Matthew 26:71, somebody else said, *"This fellow was also with Jesus of Nazareth"* This time he'll basically say, "No, I swear to God I'm not," because it says in Verse 72, *"And again he denied **with an oath**, I do not know the man."* I've been a professor for years, and there's just something about when a student says, "I swear to God I'm not cheating. I swear to God I wasn't doing anything wrong." You know they are guilty. Peter says it because he doesn't want to get caught. He doesn't want to get exposed.

Finally, Peter is confronted for the third time in Verse 73, *"Surely thou also art one of them; for thy speech bewrayeth thee."* This time, the Bible says in Matthew 26:74, *"Then began he **to curse and to swear**, saying, I know not the man."* Peter, a disciple of Christ, denies that he ever knew Jesus. Peter denies Him three times while at the House of Caiaphas, the palace of the high priest, that overlooks the Temple Mount in the distance. The statue pictured on this page tries to recreate for us that exact scene of Peter, the denier, the two women, and the Roman soldier stationed there. Peter denies Christ three times before all of them—"I don't know Him. I don't know Him. I don't know Him."

In John 18:18, it says, *"And the servants and officers stood there, who had made a fire of coals; for it was cold: and they warmed themselves: and Peter stood with them, and warmed himself."* It's there at the fire of charcoal coals that Peter stands warming his hands by the fire of the enemy, and he denies the Lord three times.

Later, in John 21:1-14, after Jesus has risen from the dead, Jesus stands on the shore of the Sea of Galilee and has a **charcoal fire**. He's prepared fish and bread, and in Verse 5, He calls to the disciples who are in a boat, *"Children, have ye any meat? They answered him, No. And he said unto them, Cast the net on the right side of the ship, and ye shall find. They cast therefore, and now they were not able to draw it for the multitude of fishes."*

Then John says to Peter in Verse 7, *"It is the Lord."* Peter jumps in the water and swims to shore. They have a meal—the last breakfast, if you will—then afterwards in John 21:15-17, Peter goes aside with Jesus. To paraphrase the passage, Jesus walks him down the beach and says, "Peter do you love me"? He replies, "Yes, Lord." Jesus asks again, "Peter, do you love me?" Peter repeats, "Yes, Lord." Then, Jesus asks again, "Peter, do you love me?" Jesus asks for three affirmations of Peter's love to counteract the three denials at the charcoal fire.

From the moment Peter got on the beach and saw the coal of fires, I think he knew what was coming. It was at the same kind of a fire that Peter had said, "I don't know You." In fact, one of the greatest verses in all of the Bible is found in Luke 22:61, which is part of Luke's account of Peter's three denials. It says, *"And the Lord turned, and looked upon Peter."*

Jesus has His back to the crowd down below, and He is facing His accusers. Upon Peter's denial, Jesus turns around, turning His back on the high priest. You don't do that if you are Jewish. Jesus looks down into the courtyard below and sees Peter. When Jesus looks upon Peter, it says in Luke 22:61-62, *"And Peter remembered the word of the Lord, how he had said unto him, Before the cock crow, thou shalt deny me thrice. And Peter went out, and wept bitterly."*

On that night, both Judas and Peter, who had been disciples of Jesus, fail the Lord miserably. Judas betrays Jesus, but Peter denies Him three times. The end result is that Judas goes out and hangs himself, while Peter repents. That was the difference.

Peter is brokenhearted. He rushes out into the night and weeps bitterly thinking, "I've failed the Lord." Later in the story, once Peter hears that Jesus is risen from the dead, he runs to the tomb and pulls up the grave clothes looking for the Savior. He is not there. Peter is there that first night when Jesus appears as the resurrected Christ. He shows the disciples

The detention facility in the House of Caiaphas complex, where prisoners would be whipped

Israeli guide, Yuval Shamesh, shows how prisoners were chained to the wall and punished at the House of Caiaphas

His hands and His feet. Peter is there when they realize Jesus is alive.

It's much later when they walk down the beach, and Jesus asks him three times, "Peter, do you love me? Do you love me? Do you love me?" In John 21:17, Peter gives his response, *"And he said unto him, Lord, thou knowest all things; thou knowest that I love thee. Jesus saith unto him, Feed my sheep."* Even after the denial, Jesus wants Peter to feed His sheep.

You may have failed the Lord yourself at sometime in your life. You may be wondering could God ever use me at all? I want to encourage you. If God could forgive and restore Peter, God can do the same for you, but it's a matter of the heart. You and I must say, "I know that I have sinned. I know that I have failed." Just as you come to Christ to receive the gift of salvation by faith, often we as believers have to receive the gift of forgiveness, as well.

Ultimately, it's not about us. It's not really about Peter. It is all about Jesus. Peter isn't the foundation of the Church. We see that Peter failed in a sense. The real Foundation and Cornerstone is Jesus Christ.

What really matters in the life of every person is that I know the Lord Jesus as my Savior, that my life is committed to Him, and that I have found real forgiveness from Him. **Only He can forgive your sin and change your life.**

Jesus Is Brought Before Pilate

It is A.D. 33, and Jesus has come to Jerusalem for the feast of Passover. Very early on Friday morning of Passover week, Jesus is being led to the Fortress of Antonia. This is the facility built by Herod that houses the Roman garrison during the pilgrim feast. The troops are here in force to keep order and to suppress any notion of an uprising.

Jesus had been arrested the night before at the Garden of Gethsemane. He was tried in the middle of the night before a hastily called meeting of priests and elders. Now, as the sun begins to rise over the city of Jerusalem, they lead Jesus to the residence of Pontus Pilate, the provincial Roman governor and only authority in the land capable of carrying out an execution. The religious leaders will petition Pilate to have Jesus put to death for what they consider blasphemy against God.

One of the most amazing stories that's ever been told in all the history of mankind is the story of the arrest, trial, and crucifixion of Jesus Christ. Jesus of Nazareth—is He just a prophet? Is He a fanatic who wants to radically revolutionize the world in some way? Or does He really believe that He is the Messiah, the Son of God, the Promised One from the Old Testament prophecies?

We read in John 18 and 19 the story of what happens after the trial before Caiaphas

The hole above is the entrance to the pit where prisoners would have been kept—the prisoners would literally be lowered into the pit through that hole

Etchings discovered in the pavement stones of Pilot's judgment hall, where the Romans soldiers would have gambled for Jesus' clothes and presented Him a crown of thorns in a cruel game called "The King's Game"

The place of the pavement refers to the pavement stones beneath the Convent of Ecce Homo—these are the actual stones of the courtyard of Pilot's judgment hall, where Jesus and other prisoners would be presented to Pilot

the high priest. That was an illegitimate trial that was conducted in the middle of the night. Early in the morning, the Bible says in John 18:28-29, *"Then led they Jesus from Caiaphas unto the hall of judgment: and it was early; and they themselves* (the priests) *went not into the judgment hall, lest they should be defiled; but that they might eat the passover. Pilate then went out unto them, and said, What accusation bring ye against this man?"*

The priests come early in the morning probably when it's just barely daybreak. They are literally waking up Pilate, the Roman governor, saying, "We need your help."

Verses 30-31 continue, *"They answered and said unto him, If he were not a malefactor, we would not have delivered him up unto thee. Then said Pilate unto them, Take ye him, and judge him according to your law. The Jews therefore said unto him, It is not lawful for us to put any man to death."*

Pilate's attitude is, "Why don't you take Him and judge Him yourself? This sounds to me like a theological controversy—a Jewish problem. It's not my problem. I'm a Roman governor." Their attitude is "No, He deserves to die, and you are the only one who can authorize putting Him to death." They are literally already committed to the

idea that Jesus needs to be crucified. They came to what then was the Antonia Fortress. The basement level of the Convent of Ecce Homo is literally over the place where Pilate will eventually say, "Behold the man," which is *Ecce Homo* in the Latin language.

In other words, Pilate will say, "Here He is. Isn't this enough? I've scourged Him, whipped Him, and beat Him half to death. Haven't you seen enough blood? Isn't that enough to let Him go." And the crowd will begin to scream, "No, crucify Him. Crucify Him."

The first-century **pavement stones** are still there. You can literally walk on the pavement that was then part of the road right on the edge of the fortress. Inside the fortress,

The western wall of the
Temple Mount in Jerusalem

The cross flower,
which mimics the shape
of a cross, blooms in Israel
in places like the Garden of Gethsemane

the place where they beat Jesus, stripped Him of His clothes, put the crown of thorns on His head, and put the purple robe on Him. Soon, they will take Him to literally be beaten half to death.

We pick the story up in John 18:33 where it says, *"Then Pilate entered into the judgment hall again, and called Jesus, and said unto him, Art thou the King of the Jews?"* In all, Pilate asks Jesus seven questions.

John was one of the two disciples that showed up at the judgment at Caiaphas' house. Again, he probably follows at a distance, but this private conversation has to be relayed later by Jesus to His disciple so that it can be recorded in the Scriptures.

During the conversation, Pilate will ask seven questions of Jesus. First of all, he says to Jesus, **"Art thou the King of the Jews?"**

Verse 34 says, *"Jesus answered him, Sayest thou this thing of thyself, or did others tell it thee of me?"* Then Pilate gets a little tense with Jesus and asks the second question, *"Pilate answered, **Am I a Jew?**"* In other words, how am I supposed to know the answer to that? This is your problem. Your people are accusing you of this thing.

Then Pilate asks Jesus, **"What hast thou done?"** This is question number three. Jesus' response to him in Verse 36 is, *"My kingdom*

there is also pavement inside where the first-century game of the king is carved right into the pavement stones. That king's game area is the place where the soldiers would gamble to determine which prisoner would be made king for the day.

Since Jesus is being accused of being the King of the Jews, it's a natural place for Him to have been brought. Undoubtedly, this is

is not of this world: if my kingdom were of this world, then would my servants fight, that I should not be delivered to the Jews: but now is my kingdom not from hence."

Jesus is saying that He hasn't come to set up a theocracy right now. He hasn't come to set up a literal Kingdom on earth. That will come at the Second Coming. But, in the First Coming, Jesus knows that He's come to suffer and die and to initiate a spiritual kingdom where Jesus wants to be Lord and Master of your life. He wants to live in your heart.

His kingdom is not of this world. That's not saying it never will be, but it wasn't to be at this point in time. He says to Pilate, "My kingdom is not of this world." In other words, I'm no threat to you at all, Pilate.

Then, in John 18:37, Pilate asked the fourth question, **"Art thou a king then?"** Jesus' response is yes—"Thou sayest that I am a king. To this end was I born, and for this cause came I into the world, that I should bear witness unto the truth. Every one that is of the truth heareth my voice."

The fifth question from Pilate comes in Verse 38, **"What is truth?"** When Pilate had said this, I sense he is pondering that himself, "What really is the truth? What's going on here?" At this point, it says, "And when he had said this, he went out again unto the Jews, and saith unto them, I find in him no fault at all." Three times Pilate will say to the leaders in Israel, "I find no fault in Him." In other words, there is no cause of putting Him to death. He is not guilty of anything. Three times Pilate will affirm that Jesus is innocent (see Luke 23:13-22).

> **Jesus came to initiate a spiritual kingdom first where He wants to be Lord and Master of your life**

This is a replica of a stone tablet bearing the name of Pontius Pilot

Then Pilate said to the crowd in Verse 39, "Will ye therefore that I release unto you the King of the Jews?" It was Passover season, and at Passover time, the custom was that the Roman governor would offer to release a prisoner as an act of goodwill to the Jewish people. We see their response in Verse 40, "Then cried they all again, saying, Not this man, but Barabbas. Now Barabbas was a robber." The crowd wants Jesus to be crucified.

In John 19, Pilate takes Jesus and scourges Him. He doesn't want to crucify Jesus. Pilate is trying to find a way out of this, and that becomes obvious in this passage. This is the time when the soldiers literally take that whip and typically give 40 lashes less one. Jesus is given 39 lashes with the Roman whip against His back with bits of glass and bone in the edges of the whip that literally rip and tear your flesh. Before Jesus ever went to the cross, He is like a piece of raw meat bleeding profusely. Pilate's idea is to beat Jesus enough and make Him bleed enough that maybe it will satisfy the crowd. If they see some blood, Pilate is hoping they'll finally say, okay, okay, release Him.

John 19:2-3 says, "And the soldiers platted a crown of thorns, and put it on his head, and they put on him a purple robe, And said, Hail, King of the Jews! and they smote him with their hands." Jesus has been defiled by the temple guards. He's been defiled by the high priest. He has been defiled by the Roman soldiers.

Here is the Son of God, who has literally become a human being in human flesh. He is fully God and yet fully human. He feels the pain. He feels the agony. He feels the rejection that He's going through. He is going through a time of torture like you and I cannot even begin to imagine.

John 19:4-5 says, *"Pilate therefore went forth again, and saith unto them, Behold, I bring him forth to you, that ye may know that I find no fault in him. Then came Jesus forth, wearing the crown of thorns, and the purple robe. And Pilate saith unto them, Behold the man!"* Pilate was standing on the balcony of his fortress looking down to the crowd on the pavement below, and he says in Latin, *"Ecce Homo,"* which means behold, the Man. Here He is. Isn't this enough? Look what we have done to Him.

Verses 6-7 say, *"When the chief priests therefore and officers saw him, they cried out, saying, Crucify him, crucify him. Pilate saith unto them, Take ye him, and crucify him: for I find no fault in him. The Jews answered him, We have a law, and by our law he ought to die, because he made himself the Son of God."*

When Pilate heard this, he walked back in the Judgment Hall, and he asked Jesus question number six. He looked to Jesus and said, *"Whence art thou?"* which means where are you from? Jesus would not answer him.

Then, in Verse 10, Pilate asked question number seven, **"Knowest thou not that I have power to crucify thee, and have power to release thee?"** Jesus looked at him and said in Verse 11, *"Thou couldest have no power at all against me, except it were given thee from above."*

> " *Our sins sent Jesus to the cross, and our sins put Him to death* "

John 19:12 says, *"Pilate sought to release him: but the Jews cried out, saying, If thou let this man go, thou art not Caesar's friend: whosoever maketh himself a king speaketh against Caesar."* In other words, you're no friend of Caesar if you release Him. You are betraying Caesar. We're all supposed to be in submission to the Roman Caesar, and you're the Roman governor, the procreator. You're his representative? What kind of a leader are you?

We know from history that Pilate has a very troubled 10 years in which he tries to serve as the governor in Judea. He doesn't understand the Jewish people. He doesn't understand their religion. He doesn't understand the Old Testament, and he certainly doesn't understand Jesus.

Finally, we see in Matthew 27:24, Pilate brings in the bowl of water—*"When Pilate saw that he could prevail nothing, but that rather a tumult was made, he took water, and washed his hands before the multitude, saying, I am innocent of the blood of this just person: see ye to it."* In other words, Pilate is trying to say, "I'm washing my hands of the whole thing. You take Him and crucify Him." However, it's Pilate's own soldiers who will take Jesus to Golgotha.

Ultimately, it's not the Jews that killed Him. It's not the Romans that killed Him. It's not even Pilate that killed Him. It's you and me. Our sins sent Jesus to the cross. Our sins put Him to death. It is as though we ourselves, as guilty sinners before God, are standing there saying, "Crucify Him."

Yet, the testimony of history is, "Jesus is innocent. I find no fault in Him."

The soldiers take Jesus down the *Via Dolorosa*—"the way of sorrows"—to Golgotha outside the gate of the city. There, outside the gate, the Scapegoat, who is the Lamb of God, will bear the sins of the whole world, and…

Jesus will die in your place and in mine!

Golgotha or the place of the skull is a rocky outcropping near the Damascus gate of the old city of Jerusalem— this is where Jesus was crucified

CHAPTER 12
HIS CRUCIFIXION & RESURRECTION

Location: Jerusalem, Circa A.D. 33

> "Then cometh Jesus with them unto a place called Gethsemane, and saith unto the disciples, Sit ye here, while I go and pray yonder. And he took with him Peter and the two sons of Zebedee, and began to be sorrowful and very heavy. Then saith he unto them, My soul is exceeding sorrowful, even unto death: tarry ye here, and watch with me. And he went a little further, and fell on his face, and prayed, saying, O my Father, if it be possible, let this cup pass from me: nevertheless not as I will, but as thou wilt."

MATTHEW 26:36-39

As we learned in previous chapters, Jesus has made His triumphal entry into the city of Jerusalem. After doing so, He openly taunted the religious authorities as He was welcomed by the crowd who greet Him as the prophesized King in the line of David. Jesus then entered the temple grounds where He argued with the temple priests and violently disrupted the exchange of money for the temple tax.

The week that celebrated the feast of Passover had barely begun when Jesus confronted representatives of all three of the leading Jewish groups in Jerusalem. He also made a startling prediction—one that shocked and angered His critics. The temple, the most sacred place in all of Judaism, is going to be destroyed. Jesus was deliberately provoking His enemies to action, and their response will be swift and deadly.

From the time of Jesus' arrest to the time He will hang on the cross will be extremely short. Jesus will hang on the cross when most people in Jerusalem are still preparing for the festival day of Passover.

We learned that Jesus was seized in the Garden of Gethsemane where He and His disciples had gathered for prayer after an early Passover meal, according to eyewitness accounts recorded in the Gospels. Under the cover of darkness, the temple guards, who were aided and directed by one of Jesus' closest followers, Judas Iscariot, arrested Jesus and led Him to the House of Caiaphas, the high priest.

The **House of Caiaphas** was not a residence as much as it was a detention facility. It was located near the temple mount, and this is where Jesus was confronted by His accusers.

A group of community elders and scribes were joined by the temple priest, and an illegal trial was held in the middle of the night. While they deliberated His fate, Jesus was held prisoner.

Gospel writers tell us that, very early in the morning, the Sanhedrin convened to formally charge Jesus with blasphemy. This Jewish court elected to take Jesus to the Roman authorities for final judgment

This mosaic of Christ is found at The Place of the Pavement in Pilot's Judgment Hall

and dispensation. The charges against Jesus, however, were changed from blasphemy to treason against the Roman government.

As the sun rose over the Mount of Olives, Jesus was taken to the **fortress of Antonia**. This was the facility built to house the Roman garrison during the pilgrim feast. It was there, in a courtyard known as the Judgment Hall, that Jesus came face to face with the Roman provincial governor, Pontius Pilate. Surprisingly, there was a crowd in the courtyard that morning—most likely one that was stirred up by the temple authorities as most of Jerusalem would have been unaware that a trail was even taking place.

Pilate had misgivings about condemning a man in whom he had found no fault. So he decided to send Jesus to Herod Antipas, the son of the late King Herod the Great. Jesus was then taken to the palace complex in upper Jerusalem where He appeared before Herod Antipas. There Jesus was mocked and adorned with what witnesses describe as a beautiful robe. Herod then sent Jesus back to Pilate.

In Chapter 11, we learned that the Roman governor was still reluctant to execute Jesus. He attempted to appease the crowd by having

Jesus beaten with a whip, which was imbedded with glass and metal. It was a painful process known as scourging.

Pilate further attempted to release another prisoner in exchange for Jesus, but the crowd wouldn't have it. Pilate was shouted down by a crowd who demanded the blood of Jesus.

"Crucify Him," they cried, and so Pilate reluctantly agreed, while famously washing his hands of what he proclaimed to be innocent blood.

It was still early in the day when Jesus was mocked by Roman soldiers and was victimized in a cruel game called *The King's Game*, where they presented Jesus with the crown of thorns and gambled for His beautiful robe.

His Crucifixion

By most accounts, it is just 9:00 a.m. when a beaten and bloodied Jesus arrives at "The Place of the Skull." It is a place of execution known as Golgotha. This is where the Rabbi from Nazareth—the Preacher, Teacher, and miracle Worker—will be will be nailed to a cross, and He will suffer and die between two criminals.

The climax to the life of Christ comes at **Golgotha**, "The Place of the Skull," a very noisy place even in first-century Jerusalem, just as it is today in the 21st century. Golgotha

is a public place where people will walk back and forth by it constantly, and a crucifixion is a public execution that is meant to literally terrorize the population into submission.

Once Pilate finally makes the decision that Jesus is to be crucified and turns Him over to the Roman soldiers, Jesus is going to die the death of a criminal. Think of that. Roman citizens could not be crucified. They had to be beheaded, which was considered an act of swift justice and mercy, but foreigners and criminals would be crucified. Jesus dies as a criminal in this place because you and I are the criminals. He takes the punishment of our sin upon Himself.

Golgotha

The Biblical account says this in Matthew 27:33, *"And when they were come unto a place called Golgotha, that is to say, a place of a skull."* The hill even has the appearance of a skull as we look at it today.

Then, the Scripture says, *"And they crucified him, and parted his garments, casting lots: that it might be fulfilled which was spoken by the prophet, They parted my garments among them, and upon my vesture did they cast lots."* In Psalm 22, the Psalm begins with the words, *"My God, my God, why hast thou forsaken me?"* These are the very words that Jesus will quote while on the cross in this place. In that same Psalm, in Verse 16, it says, *"They pierced my hands and my feet."* Then, Verse 18 says, *"They part my garments among them, and cast lots upon my vesture."*

It is obvious that David, under the inspiration of the Spirit of God, had looked down through the corridor of time a thousand years to the time that Jesus would go to the cross and die for the sins of mankind in this very public place.

Then, Matthew 27:37 says, *"And set up over his head his accusation written, THIS IS JESUS THE KING OF THE JEWS."* Perhaps sometimes you have seen a cross in a church with the letters **INRI**. The "I" stands for Jesus in the Latin language. The "N" stands for

Nazareth. The "R" is Rex for King, and the second "I" is for Jews in the Greek language. *Iēsus Nazarēnus, Rēx Iūdaeōrum* means Jesus of Nazareth, the King of the Jews.

Some of the Jews object to this. John 19:21-22 tells us, *"Then said the chief priests of the Jews to Pilate, Write not, The King of the Jews; but that he said, I am King of the Jews. Pilate answered, What I have written I have written."* I think Pilate understands that Jesus is not guilty of what the Jews accuse

Him of and feels that the Jews have virtually forced him into agreeing to the crucifixion. Yet, Pilate makes the decision, and Pilate still bears the responsibility of that decision.

Matthew 27:39-43 says, *"And they that passed by reviled him, wagging their heads, And saying, Thou that destroyest the temple, and buildest it in three days, save thyself. If thou be the Son of God, come down from the cross. Likewise also the chief priests mocking him, with the scribes and elders, said, He saved others; himself he cannot save. If he be the King of Israel, let him now come down from the cross, and we will believe him. He trusted in God; let him deliver him now, if he will have him: for he said, I am the Son of God."*

One of the great **mysteries** of the cross and one of the great powerful statements of the cross is the fact that Jesus did not come down. He willingly stays on the cross when He has the ability to call legions of angels to deliver Him. Yet, He does not do it. Why? He knew from the beginning of His earthly ministry that this is the reason that He had come into the world. He knew He would come to die for our sins and pay the price on our behalf.

The cry found in Matthew 27:46, *"Eli, Eli, lama sabachthani?* (Aramaic) *that is to say, My God, my God, why hast thou forsaken me?"* is Jesus quoting Psalm 22. It is not so much because God cannot look at Jesus on the cross, but it is because God looks at Him in wrath and judgment, even as God looks at a condemned sinner.

In that moment, Jesus feels the full weight of the wrath of God against sin, and the Bible tells us that He who knew no sin became sin for us (2 Corinthians 5:21). In other words, while on the cross, our sin is laid on Jesus, and His soul bears the weight of the judgment of God against the sin of all mankind.

Think of what that means in the terrible public place of Golgotha with the public spectacle of the crucifixion, the crowd mocking Him, and his mother weeping. Only one disciple shows up at the cross, and that's John. We read in John 19:26-27, *"When Jesus therefore saw his mother, and the disciple standing by, whom he loved, he saith unto his mother, Woman, behold thy son! Then saith he to the disciple, Behold thy mother! And from that hour that disciple took her unto his own home."*

Jesus realizes that His earthly ministry is about to come to the end. He is about to depart this world and return unto the Father, and it's there from the cross that He will ultimately stand up in triumph, as He pulls Himself up against the nails, stands up on the spikes, and shouts triumphantly, ***"It is finished."***

In the Greek New Testament, this is the word *tetelestai*. It literally means "paid in full." It's a commercial term that was often used on a contract of purchase to say "paid in full," which means the debt is paid. That is exactly what Jesus is doing on the cross. He's paying the debt on our behalf. He comes and dies in our place. He understands the significance of what is happening. Yet, in His humanity, He suffers the full weight of the physical pain of the crucifixion, and in His deity, He suffers the full judgment of the Father against our sins.

When one is hanging on a cross, imagine that the whole weight of his body is standing on the nails. You have to literally pull against spikes in your hands, and as you do a pull-up, you are gasping for breath hundreds of times, breathing through your mouth. That is why Jesus says from the cross, *"I thirst,"* as He is literally doing a pull-up on the cross over and over again in order to breathe.

While hanging from the nails on the cross, your ribs will begin to push down against your diaphragm. You can't breathe. Your knees are bent. Your heels are dug into the base of the cross. You kick your heels in to the cross and pull yourself up over and over and over again just to breathe. Plus, you're bleeding profusely.

For Jesus, His back had already been ripped open from the scourging He received from Pilate's guards. Now, His battered back pushes up and down against the cross piece. He is literally ripping the flesh on His back more and more. He is bleeding from His hands and from His feet, as well as from the crown of thorns on His head. Yet, the greatest judgment of all is the impact of our sin that is now laid upon Him.

It's really not the Jews or the Romans who crucified Him—it's you and me. It's our sin that sent Jesus to the cross, and He bears the judgment of God on our behalf.

The Garden Tomb in east Jerusalem

JESUS CHRIST DECLARED WITH POWER (TO BE THE SON OF GOD BY THE RESURRECTION FROM THE DEAD ROMANS 1:4

Inside the Garden Tomb we see the place where Jesus may have been laid

For a victim of **crucifixion**, in those terrible moments when exhaustion finally overtakes you, you collapse and cannot push yourself up to breathe any longer. At that point, ultimately your heart bursts from suffocation. That is what happens to Jesus. He dies from His heart bursting. In that moment during that powerful heart attack when all of a sudden Jesus' human life comes to an end, Luke 23:46 says, *"And when Jesus had cried with a loud voice, he said, Father, into thy hands I commend my spirit: and having said thus, he gave up the ghost."*

That moment of judgment is the judgment that you and I should have borne on the cross, but Jesus did it on our behalf. Against all of the noise, the racquet, and the screaming of the crowd, Jesus goes to the cross because He loves us.

His Burial

The Rabbi from Nazareth, who was arrested under cover of darkness, tried in the middle of the night, and then hurried to the cross, will not be left for public spectacle.

According to all four Gospel writers, **Joseph of Arimathea**, an honorable man, will generously donate his tomb for the burial of Jesus. It is believed that Joseph, who is a member of the Sanhedrin, is indeed a secret follower of Jesus.

Joseph boldly goes to Pontius Pilate and asks for the body to be removed from the cross and given over to him for a proper burial. Pilate complies, and the body of Jesus is taken to Joseph's family tomb, which is conveniently located in a garden very near the place of execution.

The body of Jesus is quickly washed and wrapped in a shroud. Those who tend to this task must complete their work before the sun sets because the *Shabbat* or the Sabbath day will begin.

The body of Jesus is placed in the tomb, and the tomb is sealed. The body of Jesus will rest in this tomb on the Sabbath day.

His Resurrection

The resurrection of Jesus Christ is the most powerful event in all of human history. It's the event that changes everything. His death atones for our sin, but His resurrection from the dead gives Him the ability to give us the gift of eternal life. It's His triumph over the power of Satan.

The Bible tells us in Genesis 3:15 that ultimately the seed of the woman, which means somebody who will step into the human race, will crush the head of the serpent. Yet, in the process, He will bruise His heel. *"And I will put enmity between thee and the woman, and between thy seed and her seed; it shall bruise thy head, and thou shalt bruise his heel."* Crucifixion victims literally

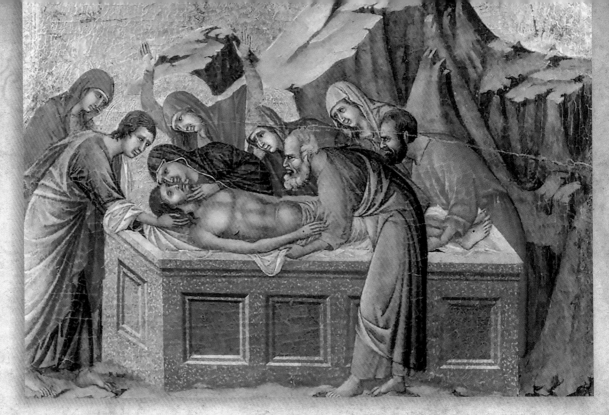

bruise their heels against the base of the cross, ripping the flesh off the heels.

After His death on the cross, Jesus' body is then wrapped in the shroud. It's brought to the new tomb of Joseph of Arimathea. It is laid there. All the disciples assume this is the end. He is dead. They understand the seriousness of crucifixion and what it means. You don't walk away from something like that. All hope seems to be lost.

Yet, on Sunday morning, the first day of the week, the women come back to the tomb wanting again to anoint the body with spices and finish the burial properly. Shockingly, they discover that the **stone is rolled away**. This was not done to let Jesus out of the tomb, but instead to let us into the tomb so that everyone can see He is not here. He is risen, as He said.

In Luke 24:1-6 says: *"Now upon the first day of the week, very early in the morning, they came unto the sepulchre (the tomb), bringing the spices which they had prepared, and certain others with them. And they found the stone rolled away from the sepulchre. And they entered in, and found not the body of*

Another view of the Garden Tomb

the Lord Jesus. And it came to pass, as they were much perplexed thereabout, behold, two men stood by them in shining garments (two angels): And as they were afraid, and bowed down their faces to the earth, they said unto them, Why seek ye the living among the dead? He is not here, but is risen."

The people at the tomb begin to scatter and leave. However, **Mary Magdalene** lingers behind. It's there that Jesus appears to her. She thinks that He's the gardener and in John 20:15 says, *"Sir, if thou have borne him hence, tell me where thou hast laid him."* Suddenly Jesus speaks to her in that familiar voice and tone in Verse 16, *"Mary."* She then realizes it's Him. She wants to run to Him to grab Him because she's so thrilled and excited that He's alive. Yet, He has to say in Verse 17, *"Touch me not; for I am not yet ascended to my Father: but go to my brethren, and say unto them, I ascend unto my Father, and your Father; and to my God, and your God."*

The women run back to the city to let the disciples know He's risen, but the disciples don't believe it. Finally, Peter and John run to the tomb. When they get there, John appropriately bends down and looks into the tomb, but Peter rushes inside the tomb and starts picking up all the grave clothes looking for the body. Peter is verifying that Jesus is not here—He's gone.

It's later that day when the Bible tells us Jesus begins to appear to the disciples. Luke 24:13 says, *"And, behold, two of them went that same day to a village called Emmaus, which was from Jerusalem about threescore furlongs."* Jesus suddenly appears and walks along with them.

He talks to them about what has happened in Jerusalem, and they say to Him in Verses 19-20, *"Concerning Jesus of Nazareth, which was a prophet mighty in deed and word before God and all the people: And how the chief priests and our rulers delivered him to be condemned to death, and have crucified him."*

As they talk, Jesus reminds them in Verse 26, *"Ought not Christ to have suffered these things, and to enter into his glory?"* In other

> *Jesus dares to say that all of the Old Testament—the prophecies, types, pictures, and symbols—are about Him*

words, Isaiah 53 has to be fulfilled. The **suffering Servant** must die for our sins before the resurrection and before His glorification, when He reigns and rules as King in our hearts and lives.

Luke 24:27 continues, *"And beginning at Moses and all the prophets, he expounded unto them in all the scriptures the things concerning himself."* What a Bible study! Jesus is the teacher.

The two arrive in **Emmaus** with Jesus and still don't realize with whom they have been speaking. They invite Him to dinner and are ready to have the meal together. Luke 24:30-31 says, *"And it came to pass, as he sat at meat with them, he took bread, and blessed it, and brake, and gave to them. And their eyes were opened, and they knew him; and he vanished out of their sight."*

When Jesus appears to the disciples again later and has another meal with them, Luke 24:44 says, *"And he said unto them, These are the words which I spake unto you, while I was yet with you, that all things must be fulfilled, which were written in the* **law** *of Moses, and in the* **prophets***, and in the* **psalms***, concerning me."*

Suddenly, their eyes are opened, and they realize it's Him. Jesus explains that all things must be fulfilled—not some things and not most things. All things must be fulfilled that are written in three places—the Law of Moses, the prophets, and the Psalms. That's the threefold designation of the *Tanakh*, which is the Old Testament of the Hebrew Scriptures.

In other words, Jesus dares to say that all of the Old Testament is ultimately all about Me. He is there in all the prophecies, the types, the pictures, and the symbols of the Old Testament. The Old Testament is pointing to the Lamb of sacrifice, to the atonement that needs to be

A faithful Jew prays at the Wailing Wall in Jerusalem

made, to the blood that needs to be shed, and to the Priest who makes the offering. All of those are pictures of Christ. He is the High Priest. He is the atoning sacrifice. He is the Lamb of God. He is the risen Savior, and Luke 24:45 says, *"Then opened he their understanding, that they might understand the scriptures."*

His Commission

In that powerful passage in Luke 24, the risen Christ appears to them, reveals Himself to them, and then the commission is given. Luke 24:47-48 says, *"And that repentance and remission of sins should be preached in his name among all nations, beginning at Jerusalem. And ye are witnesses of these things."* And Matthew 28:19-20 says, *"Go ye therefore, and teach all nations, baptizing them in the name of the Father, and of the Son, and of the Holy Ghost: Teaching them to observe all things whatsoever I have commanded you: and, lo, I am with you alway, even unto the end of the world. Amen."*

We are to preach the Gospel unto **all nations** and tell everyone the Good News—that sin is atoned for, that the Savior is risen, and that the victory is won!

What a wonderful thing that we can stand at the garden tomb at this beautiful place in the land of Israel. It commemorates the resurrection of the Savior. Yet, our faith is

A statue of Jesus and Peter at the Sea of Galilee presumably at the location where Jesus appeared to Peter and the disciples

not based the stones of the tomb. Our faith is based on a living Savior. He is alive today and wants to live in your heart and in your life. He is willing to come in, and by the power of His Holy Spirit, He gives us the opportunity of new birth.

Remember, in John 3:3, Jesus said to Nicodemus, *"Except a man be born again, he cannot see the kingdom of God."* In John 19:38-42, we read that, at the end of Jesus' earthly life, it's Nicodemus who is there professing his faith in Christ, and it's Joseph of Arimathea, a disciple of Jesus. They are there showing their commitment to Jesus when they bury Him. Yet, what a stunning surprise it is when they all learn that Jesus is not in the tomb. He is risen, as He said.

Yes, His death is essential and important because it reminds us that He died for us, but it's His resurrection that convinces us He is indeed the Son of God. He is the One who alone can give to you and me the gift of eternal life. Jesus Himself said earlier in John 6:47, *"Verily, verily, I say unto you, He that believeth on me hath everlasting life."*

We can study the life of Christ. We can be amazed at His teaching, such as the beauty and power of the Sermon on the Mount. We can be stunned by His wisdom as He upstages all of His critics and shows them what the Law of Moses is really all about. He teaches us what the message of God really meant in both the Old Testament and ultimately in the New Testament. More than anything else, we have to come face to face with **Jesus the person**.

The question is: Is He really who He said He is? Is He a liar who claimed He is the Son of God? Is He a lunatic who thought He is the Son of God, or is He Lord and Master because He really is the Son of God? You can reject Him as a heretic as so many have. You can pity Him as a lunatic, or you can

bow your knees before Him and can cry, "My Lord and my God."

In all, Jesus will appear 10 times and will be seen in His resurrected form by hundreds of witnesses over a 40-day period after Passover. He appears to His disciples in Jerusalem. He directs them to a mountain in Galilee where As we have seen, He appears and challenges His followers to carry the Gospel—the Good News—to all nations.

He appears to those who believe and to those who doubt. One appearance is to Thomas, His disciple, the skeptical servant, who places his own hand into Jesus' side to feel the wounds of the cross.

We learned about one of the most memorable appearances, which is to the disciples by the Sea of Galilee. These men had returned home after their tumultuous days in Jerusalem. They have come back, at least for a moment, to a life that was once familiar. Peter declares that he is going fishing and is joined by several other disciples. They fish all night, but catch nothing.

Morning reveals what appears to be a Stranger on the shore. He calls out to the disciples asking if they have caught anything. When the reply is no, the Stranger tells them to cast their nets on the other side of the boat. They do this and find the fish they have been looking for. Now they know that the One who has called out to them is none other than Jesus Himself.

Peter leaps into the water and begins to swim to shore. The others follow dragging their nets full of fish. On the shore, Jesus is making preparations for breakfast. He waits for Peter by a coal fire, which is reminiscent of the one where Peter warmed his hands and denied his Master three times in Jerusalem.

Jesus will forgive Peter for this transgression, and He will challenge Peter to lead the early church. Jesus will ask the disciples to follow Him—even unto death.

These men are chosen for a very special purpose. They will eventually travel throughout the ancient world and proclaim that Jesus is the Messiah, the Suffering Servant, whose coming was foretold by the prophets of Israel. They have been **eyewitnesses** to history and will testify to Jesus' miracles and tell of those incredible days in Jerusalem when Jesus was tried and crucified, but not defeated. They will tell of the One who vanquished death as He stepped out of His tomb that He offers eternal life for all who will believe and follow Him.

Under persecution, imprisonment and even martyrdom, these disciples will hold fast to their conviction that…

Jesus is indeed the Son of God.

Sunrise over the Ascension Tower, which marks the place where Jesus ascended into heaven